TAKING STEPS

HELEN SIMS

DEDICATION

This book is dedicated to my family, friends, Anne Rogers, and all the NHS professionals that work so hard, despite often being underappreciated.

FOREWORD

From the start, things were stacked against me. I was a premature baby, born at seven months old. That alone meant my chances weren't good. I was tiny, weighing less than a bag of sugar. I could fit easily into my parents' hands, but, thanks to a series of 'unfortunate events', it would be a long time before either of them would hold their baby daughter.

Soon after my somewhat eager entrance in to the world, I was taken, as 'prem' babies are, to the Intensive Care Unit, and placed in an incubator. I will tell you, to the best of my knowledge (through what Mum has told me) and ability, about the events that happened next, and how they would change my life…forever.

My first few days were anxious. My tiny body struggled to hold onto life and my parents could do nothing but watch.

I was looked after by a wonderful team of doctors and nurses who did everything they could for me. Somehow, though, I caught an infection. All I know is that this infection developed into septicaemia and I now needed a blood transfusion.

My parents waited.

I came through it.

Over the next few days, I was returned to my incubator wrapped in bubble wrap, (very fetching!) and attached to a heart monitor. Mum was relieved. "She's come through this; surely nothing else can go wrong, can it?" – But it did.

The heart monitor I had been linked up to showed no problems and was beeping reassuringly, as always, but … I wasn't breathing!

It had been a busy shift. Doctors were trying, (and ultimately failing) to save a baby boy in a cot near mine. Luckily a passing nurse noticed something was wrong with me.

It was a battle to save me but "I began to breathe again. My mum cried. I was alive but I had already paid the price, and my life had been changed forever.

In those minutes that I was 'dead', no oxygen was reaching my brain, and the parts that control my mobility were damaged. I was nine days old.

Cerebral Palsy affects its sufferers in different ways. Some can't talk or walk, some have learning difficulties. I know I got off lightly. But it's been a long, hard road, getting to where I am now.

Until I was eight, I attended a 'special school' that was attached to the hospital where I was born. It was a cosy, happy, safe place. I had a lot of friends and many of the teachers there called me "Miss Sunshine".

It became obvious to my parents that I needed more. I could do more.

All I knew was that there were days when I would finish the work early, and I was able to sit at my desk and write stories. I loved that, but what I loved more was helping the other children. They were my friends and we were, all in the same boat. I was not different.

I had many friends that were much worse off than I was. My best friend, Milly, was a lovely little blonde girl with the most beautiful blue eyes I have ever seen in my life. 'Milly' couldn't walk or talk. She talked to me though. We developed a code. She used her hands, eyes, and facial movements to tell me things. I'd ask her a question and she would indicate yes or no with her left and right hands. Most importantly to me though, she was Milly. She would laugh with me ... although sometimes, I knew she laughed at me! I would spend playtimes, despite my difficulties walking, pushing her around in her chair. I was nothing special, I just loved being with my friends.

The day I left to go to my local 'mainstream' primary school broke my heart. Saying "goodbye" to Milly was hard, because she couldn't tell me she understood. Her eyes said she did though. I never saw Milly again.

I started my new school a month or so before my parents' separation.

I was the only person there with a disability, and for a long time children stared at me. I was different. One of the things I hated most was assembly. While the other children sat cross legged on the floor, I had to sit to the side, on a chair. Crossing my legs caused me pain. It still does.

Eventually though, things settled down a bit and I found my niche. I was 'skipping rope holder' at play time. Part of me felt wonderful; so pleased and relieved that they wanted me to play with them. But it hurt too. I wanted to be the one skipping or playing hopscotch, and I hated being left out of 'kiss chase'. However, I understood that it was just the way things had to be. There was, there is, no choice.

At age eleven, I moved over the road to the local secondary school. Again, I was the only one with a disability. I was a different 'fish,' and this time, I was in an even larger pond. Now, though, I didn't feel so alone, because a lot of my friends came with me.

P.E. lessons were always the worst. I was timekeeper, or whistle blower. "Count the cricket bats as you hand them out, Helen." It was all the teachers could do. It wasn't their fault. I had to be included.

It also wasn't their fault that I would frequently go to the girls' toilets, lock the door, and sob my heart out.

In time I discovered that there were things I was good at, things I could really do.

I had always loved writing stories, but it was around this time that my wonderful English teacher, suggested I write a poem. I rolled my eyes, smiled, and said, "Yeah. It'll never work!" She just smiled back at me and replied, "We'll see…"

Apart from writing, my participation in P.E lessons had taken a new, more exciting twist. No, it wasn't a tall, dark and handsome teacher in shorts! Instead, it was dance lessons!

"Well, that should be her idea of hell, shouldn't it?" I hear you say. But it wasn't! I became a choreographer. I would devise the dance moves and routines for my group. "Can you just move your leg up a little higher? Hold tighter! Ok, start again!" I loved it! Teachers would come to watch, and people actually wanted ME to become part of their group!

Just when things were starting to get better, my condition, as the doctors had predicted, began to get worse. For many years I had been in a wheelchair for some of the time, but now it became a virtually permanent thing. I knew it would happen. Puberty had made my body heavier and so the strain on my already painful hips and knees became worse. This increased pain was unbearable.

It was time for 'The Surgery'.

I can't even begin to tell you how terrified I was. The hospital was 100 miles away from my home in Somerset. It was 'the best' place for me to be. I knew it would involve at least three operations and I knew I would be away for at least three months.

The first one of these operations took place on July 4th 1995. A family friend called it 'Helen's Independence Day.' I wanted to crawl under a stone, and die. "Just think of how wonderful it will be when it's all over," Mum said. I smiled and said, "Oh, okay."

During the first operation, the doctors had to break and reset my left hip so that it was in the 'right' position. They put a big plate in my hip to help the bones heal. The plate had to stay there. Also during that same operation, they put a screw in my left ankle, to help it take weight. The screw has to stay there too.

I don't remember much about after the operation, just snippets, and pain.

But the pain and the events following the second operation, I will never forget.

It took place two weeks after the first, and it involved...cutting muscles.

The doctors had to cut the muscles on and behind my knees in both legs, and also cut the muscles just above my hips. Again, in both legs.

I woke up after the operation and immediately, to put it bluntly, wished that I'd died on the table. All I could see was a red haze, and the pain was...well, it wasn't pain, it was agony. I can't describe it to you so I hope you don't mind if I don't even try! I just know that I'll never forget it.

Mum says I opened my eyes, looked at her, squeezed her hand and passed out again. The next few weeks are what I call my 'lost period.'

I was attached to a morphine drip, still in pain and in and out of consciousness.

One day though, I had the strangest experience. I woke up and I was above my body, staring down at myself. I could see my parents on either side of my bed and me, lying there, pale.

I remember clearly being able to see Robbie, a boy in the next bay that I had made friends with. He was talking to the nurses. The next thing I knew I was back inside my body, and holding my Mum's hand.

Soon, my rehabilitation began. I had to learn to walk from scratch, the 'right' way.

It was hard. There was day after day of physiotherapy, exercise classes, hydrotherapy, pain and more pain. I didn't even get a break when I was asleep. I had to wear these long blue splints that went from the top of my hips, right down to my ankles, and I had to sleep on my tummy. If I tried to change position, a nurse would come and flip me back again. They really must have had eyes in the back of their heads!

Eventually, it was time for the dreaded 'bars'. They ran parallel to each other, and I had to walk down the middle and get to the chair at the other end. Every step was long, slow, painful, and so very frustrating. "Come on Helen, you can do it! Just one more!" I wanted to break down and cry. Frequently, I did.

It was around this time that I started to lose pieces of myself. My hair had gone grey and I had already lost weight, but then things got very bad.

I was only seeing my family at weekends. Life had to go on for them and they had jobs to do, so they had to go home during the week. When they arrived on Saturday mornings, I was awful to them. I resented them for leaving me and going back to normal. After all, I couldn't. I was stuck. I resented them when they came, but I resented them more when they would kiss me goodbye and leave on a Sunday night.

I was a shell of the person I used to be. I hated myself. I hated the situation. I felt hopeless and pathetic. I didn't eat very much, and when I did, there were times when I would make myself sick. I can't explain it, but it went on for a while.

One day, the Sister took me into her office to speak to me.

"Helen, you can't keep doing this. If you do…you'll die. I know this is hard, but you need your strength. I don't want to have to put you on a drip, love."

I was still reeling. I didn't want to die. No, I didn't want to die there.

Somehow, I managed to get it together for the last 'push' as Sister called it. I just wanted to go home. I wanted to see, dad, my friends, my cat and, scarily, I wanted to get back to school.

It was hard but when I left hospital a month later, I was walking with a frame. The operations didn't turn out to be the 'miracle cure' my head and heart had hoped for but, I wasn't in a wheelchair anymore! A few months later, after a lot more physiotherapy, I was able to ditch my frame with its go faster stripes, and use crutches instead.

Life is tough, and I get frustrated. I get sad that I don't get a rest from it, and I've been stuck with it, through no fault of my own. And yes, I get angry. There are days when I just crumple in my husband's arms and cry like a baby.

People often ask me, 'If you could wave a magic wand, would you change it?' On days when I'm depressed or in pain, yes of course I would! I would give anything to be able to carry my dinner across the room, go for a long walk with my husband, or run up a flight of stairs, but more often than not, I know it helps to make me who I am.

What I've been through makes me a better person (I hope). I see people as people rather than their illness, job, or wealth. No one deserves to be treated as *just* a number on a page. Each person has a story and a life experience, and it's all worth listening to.

That is where this government is going wrong. They don't see us as individuals. To them, we are a seemingly worthless 'problem' group of people who don't fit where society (and the government) wants us to. That is not our fault! I certainly wouldn't choose to be in this situation. I don't think anybody would.

Since I am though, I am determined to try and do something good with it. I want to turn all the bad things into something positive. I want to help increase understanding of the difficulties that disabled and ill people face on a daily basis.

Disabled and ill people aren't 'scroungers' or a 'drain on society'. We have been through more, and continue to go through more, than most people can imagine. We are all a part of society and deserve to be treated with respect and dignity, just as everyone else is.

My life is worth something, despite what this government would have me (and the rest of society) believe.

I have been a disability rights campaigner (at different levels, when able, of course), since I was eight years old (twenty seven years), and I will go on fighting for as long as I have to.

Having said that though, I want this book to be about the writing (as well as raising awareness), and there is a part of me that really hopes it will stand for itself. I want to turn all negatives into positives. After all, life really is what you make it!

PLEASE

Please,
Help me,
Can't you see,
How this is making me feel?
You don't listen,
You don't care,
Why is life so unfair?

You don't know the tears I've cried,
In a silent
Empty room,
I wake up to loneliness,
Emptiness,
Doom.

There has to be gold,
At the end of the rainbow,
Please,
Tell me so,
There has to be a way to let go.

I must wake up,
Find sunshine,
Not rain,
Please,
Don't put me through this again.

Life is better than before,
I've found an open door,
Thank you for making me see,
There's something special,
Deep inside me.

SLEEPLESS

The night curls itself around me
A warm blanket
On cold Earth
Sleep will not be found tonight.

Staring into darkness,
I find myself that way,
Laughter is thought of,
A fleeting glimpse
Of the sun,
As my tears fall
And freeze,
The sound of bells,
And wind in trees.

The night wraps itself around me,
A warm blanket
For a crowded mind.

Sleep has burnt
And light is dead,
Dreams are thought of,
As the tears fall
And dry,
A perfect shape,
Of another life.

SUNRISE

I am waiting
For sunrise,
A nip has chilled
The air,
And darkness
Fills my soul.

I am waiting
For sunrise,
A distant dream
It seems,
In fever haunted nights.

I am aching
For sunrise,
A moment of peace,
Relief,
As pain becomes
A friend.

I am aching
For sunrise,
The warmth
And healing power,
Now lives
A world away,
And I am dying
Hour by hour.

At last I feel
The sunrise,
First rays
Dance over my skin.

At last I feel
The sunrise,
White night
Becomes
Day grey,
And I am ready
To live,
Again.

Now I see
My sunrise,
Tears refresh
The eyes.

Now I see
My sunrise,
A light breeze
Has filled
The air,
I live for this,
I stand
And smile,
It's time for me
To fly.

THE PRICE OF FAME

(Dedicated to Karen Carpenter 1950-1983)

The sweetest voice,
The private pain,
Her eyes said it all
The price of fame.

Her body screamed,
She yearned to be thin,
A manifestation
Of torture within.

Singing songs
Of hearts broken,
In beautiful tune,
Her words were spoken.

Stage lights shone
From up above,
See the fragile figure,
Who longed to be loved.

The public smile,
The private scream,
Her desperate struggle,
To live the dream.

On that last day,
Her heart attacked,
The agony revealed,
The mirror cracked.

The sweetest voice,
The private pain,
Her death said it all,
The price of fame.

THE ROAD TO NOWHERE

I've been walking a long time,
Thinking of you,
There is only one thing I want you to do,
Just look at the stars,
Remember I care,
It's hard out here on the road to nowhere.

If I could be there,
Believe me,
I would,
I'd be right back with you,
As fast as I could,
You've got to keep smiling,
And remember I care,
It's Hell out here on the road to nowhere.

Keep your head up to the heavens above,
Always remember there's a world full of love,
Forget about me,
If you dare,
It's Hell out here on the road to nowhere.

Now I'm with you,
Home at last,
Forget the lonely days,
They're in the past,
Just look at the sky,
And remember I care,
We'll stand together,
On the road to nowhere.

SLIPPED

I've slipped
I am shipped,
To the middle
Of a distant sea.

I've fallen,
And I'm all in
Drowned in things,
That can never be.

I am frail
And I fail,
Pain stabs me
Like a knife.

I am crying
Just left lying,
No hope
Of a better life.

I had slipped
Wings clipped,
I wanted
To get away.

I was lame
Then you came,
And you
Asked me to stay.

I was broken
Words unspoken,
You could never

Understand.

I'm me
And now I see,
You offered
Me your hand...

HELLO LITTLE EARTHLINGS

Hello Little Earthlings,
I've come from outer space,
I'm down here
On a mission,
To inspect
The human race.

Hello Little Earthlings,
I've been watching you,
I've come to try
To understand,
Why you do the things
You do.

Hello Little Earthlings,
I've seen hungry children cry,
I'm down here
From another place,
I need to ask you
Why?

Hello Little Earthlings,
I see your people are at war,
I'm curious,
And I'd like to know,
What do you do
This for?

Hello Little Earthlings,
Who kill animals just for fun,
I wish you knew
How it felt,
I'd like to see

You run!

Hello Little Earthlings,
I've seen cities choked with cars,
I've come here
And I want to know
How it got
This far?

Hello Little Earthlings,
You chop down beautiful trees,
I'm new here
And ask you why,
You bring your planet
To its knees?

Hello Little Earthlings,
I'm from a quiet,
Gentle place.
Somehow,
I think it's you that should
Inspect
The human race.

THE REJECT DOLL

I've always been a reject doll
Left alone at night,
I'm the reject doll,
My legs don't work right.

The reject doll's in the window
Watching the world go by,
I have a lopsided smile
I can't cry.

I'm the reject doll,
Tossed to one side,
Friends said they cared,
They lied.

I've always been the reject doll,
Lift me up,
Put me down
See my wobbly legs,
Throw me on the ground.

I know that I'm a reject doll,
I've always been that way,
Listen to the reject doll
She has a lot to say.

Now I'm not a reject doll,
It's taken time,
But now I'm there,
I'm no longer the reject doll,
I've found someone who cares.

Now I'm not a reject doll,

There's a peace that lies in me,
The lonely little reject doll,
Can smile,
And know she's free.

AUDITION

Alice Rose,
She chewed her nails,
Thought nervously,
What if she failed?
Inside her chest,
Her heart beat faster,
What would she do,
If they didn't cast her?

In the mirror,
A face stared back,
So tired and ugly,
The mirror should crack.
Minutes later,
Make-up on,
One false move,
Her dream was gone.

Sometime later,
And on the bus,
She peered out,
At the daytime rush,
Rain drenched roads,
And clouds of grey,
One way or other,
This was her day.

Around the corner
Up stone steps,
This was it,
'No regrets'.
Patiently she waited,
Then her moment came,

An auburn haired lady
Called her name.

A second of panic,
What if she froze?
A shiver ran
Head to toes.
Seconds later,
Through heavy doors,
A painted white room
With wooden floors.

Looking over,
She could have cried,
As they stared back,
Through empty eyes.
She remembered the lines
And spoke with feeling,
Shaking hands,
Her nerves revealing.

The moment over,
The audition done,
Her throat was dry
Was she the one?
She felt as if,
She had run a mile,
But still somehow,
She managed a smile.

Passing back
Through those heavy doors,
Her heels clicked,
Upon the floor.
Down stone steps

Onto the street,
She sat a while,
On dampened seat.

The traffic passed,
The headlights glowed,
Reflecting on
The rain drenched road.
Sometime later,
And on the bus,
Her blue eyes twinkled,
Her face was flushed.

Certain that she'd done her best,
A second's thought
For all the rest,
Desperate now,
For a cup of tea,
'Hope they feel as happy as me'.
Minutes later,
Back at her flat,
To a pile of bills
And a sleeping cat.

Five days past,
Feeling down,
Still in slippers
And her dressing gown,
The moggy lay
Across her lap,
An envelope fell
Through the letter flap.
Quickly she tore
The paper apart,
Trying to calm

Her pounding heart,
Her throat was dry,
Her eyes still tired,
Surprise,
It said,
'Miss Rose, you're hired!'

ALWAYS THERE

I have lived so long with pain.
It rips and tears at my body,
Sharp and relentless,
I know
It will always be there.

I try to be strong.
I smile as expected,
But inside I'm breaking
Apart.

When you look at me,
All you see
Is the outside,
A shell,
My disability.

I hide the agony
Deep inside,
A body that betrays me,
And it will
Always be there.

But
I am a person just like you,
I laugh and love,
I cry and need,
When I'm cut
I bleed.

I wish it was easy
And wish it would change,
The world still thinks

I'm strange.

Sometimes in darkness,
I want to scream
At tired
Frustration's flame.

And then I want the world to know,
Deep down,
I am the same.

CAN YOU SEE ME?

For a few precious moments
I escape,
Into my perfect world.
I'm drifting
Clad in silver
Over a vast ice rink.
I don't feel
I don't think.
I'm right there,
Can you see me?
The real ice queen
I was meant to be.

For a few precious moments
I escape,
Into my perfect world.
I'm singing
This time,
Centre stage
Radio City Music Hall.
I'm up there,
Can you see me?
I'm having a ball!

For a few precious moments
I escape
Into perfect world
I'm dancing
In a red dress,
A smile is on my face,
And,
Just because I can,
I'm dancing in the rain.

I'm out there,
Can you see me?
I'm where I want to be.

For a few precious moments
We have escaped
Into our perfect world.
We're standing
Holding hands
In a field of perfect green.
We laugh,
And,
Just because he can,
He gently kisses my cheek.
Can you see us?
We're still in there,
But,
This is no daydream.

TO WHOM IT MAY CONCERN

You make me want to scream sometimes,
You make me feel like I shouldn't have air,
And now I think I'm cross
Because I shouldn't even care.

You make me want to yell sometimes,
You make me feel like it's not worth trying,
And now you know what annoys me most,
Is that I'm the one who's crying!

You make me want to shout sometimes,
You make me feel like I don't have air
And now you know what hurts me most,
Is that you don't even care...

HIC-CHOO!

This germ is cunning,
My nose is running,
It's got me through and through,
It's your fault,
It really is,
I caught it from you!

My head is spinning,
This germ is winning,
I've taken to my bed,
I wish that he would leave me alone,
And bother someone else, instead!

My body aches,
I've got the shakes,
This germ has a hold you see,
I'm lying here,
With tissues near,
Oh, why is it always me?

I can't fight off
The terrible cough,
This germ, he's pounding me,
I hope that soon
He will pack his bags,
And leave me to be free!

My throat's stopped burning,
And head's stopped turning,
The germ has finally moved out,
I'm back drinking tea,
Feeling more like me,
It's so nice to be up and about!

My nose has unblocked,
My chest is unlocked,
And now I smile again,
The germ of course,
Is still in my thoughts,
Though he has gone away.
I know that it's bad,
But I am glad,
He's found somewhere else to stay!

BEAUTIFUL MUSIC

Notes pierce the darkness
Someone plays,
In beautiful music,
A memory stays.

In eerie gloom
I stand and wait,
Minutes are agony,
You are always late.

In stifling darkness
I sit alone
And stare into flames,
You will never
Come home.

Valentine's roses,
A heart of red,
Wasted and withering,
You,
Are dead.

HAPPINESS

Happiness is waking up with you
As the sun streams through our curtains,
Spending Sundays
As they should be,
Time just being us.

Happiness is autumn leaves
Spread out on the grass,
Noticing colours
Instead of grey.

Happiness is looking at the stars
On a moonlit night,
The feeling that they could have been,
Put there just for me.

Happiness is the newly made bed
After a difficult day,
Snug and warm,
And safe.

Happiness is going for a walk
Watching children play,
They laugh
And run,
All that matters
Is now.

Happiness is warmth,
It's love,
It's peace,
It's perfect moments inside myself,
That I have had to find

Happiness is all the little things,
That help to make me free.

THE ROSE

If you can
Could you take away my thorns?
They aren't nice
And I don't want them
Anymore.

As for my petals
You can notice those,
They're the pretty part
But,
When you pick me up,
Be careful not to scratch yourself.
What's above
Isn't always what's beneath...

When I wilt,
Keep my petals in a box,
They will remind you of me.

IF YOU HAD EVERYTHING

If you had everything,
Where would I be?
Getting used to the fact,
That you wouldn't need me.

If you had everything,
Where would I go?
Forget about the pain,
And 'on with the show'.

If you had everything,
What would I see?
Left all alone,
With the mirror
And me.

If you had everything,
How would it seem?
Pull myself together,
And give up a dream.

If you had everything,
You'd never know
How much you'd miss me,
When I got up to go.

If you had everything,
What would you do?
Left all alone,
With the mirror
And you.

If you had everything,
How would it feel?
Living out your days,
As if they weren't real.

Now we have everything,
We're so close
Standing here together,
Luckier than most.

Now we have everything,
Things stay as they must
Being here together,
With the mirror,
And us.

THE LIFE OF JANUARY

January stands alone,
The little boy,
No one wants
To invite into their home.

He waits there,
As the lights come down
His pale face,
Becomes a frown,

"I hate myself,
Can't you see?
Your misery
Is because of me."

January watches,
Through hollow eyes
No one cares,
Or hears his cries.

He is lonely,
All colour gone
His sad days,
Seem so long.

January is lost,
He needs a friend
But raw fingers,
Won't extend.

He dies alone
But understands,
As February comes

To take his hand...

SILENCE

Silence
Calms the soul,
I once dreaded the nothingness,
But now,
I have found
Its beauty.

Silence
Is a butterfly
Floating through the air,
I can feel a connection,
I can find myself there.

Silence
Is a dancer,
She moves
With grace,
I stand still
And watch,
The peace on her face.

Take my hand,
Come to find it,
In a crazy world,
Silence can be everywhere,
If you let it
Fill your soul.

MY BEST FRIEND

She is the girl
Everyone wanted to be,
It has always been her,
And never been me.

Blonde and blue eyed,
It's no surprise,
When all the men
Look at her twice.

Luscious long hair
Hangs round her face,
Not even an eyelash
Falls out of place.

Infectious laughter
And radiant smile,
Leave both the men
And the women beguiled.

As for boobs,
Seems she got my share,
Surprised she can walk,
With the weight of her pair!

"Hello," ignore me,
Just the ugly friend,
Always the strong one,
On which she depends.

Males absorbed
By her model pout,
Or it could just be

That her butt's hanging out!

I know she is perfect,
I hear the applause,
Let me wait here,
And sharpen my claws.

You know I love her,
But I'm down on my knees,
She's driven me crazy,
Someone slap her please!

FRIENDS FOREVER

I've always been there for you,
Now I don't care what you do.
When you need to talk,
Don't turn to me,
'Cause I've had enough,
You'll see.

The way you treat,
Is hardly fair,
You phone me up
Pretending to care.

This is what happens,
When friendship's stretched,
The fun we had together,
On my mind is etched.
We'd have our little girly talks
And cry our eyes out,
On very long walks.
We both got drunk on New Year's Eve,
The things we talked about,
You'd never believe...

Friends we said,
Friends forever,
I bet you think you're really clever.
You can kiss my boyfriend
Behind my back,
Suppose you think you've fooled the Jack.

The way I feel,
Angry and hurt,
I hope soon enough

47

Your bubble bursts.

I've had enough of your little lies,
Phoning me up
And making me cry.

Though telling me made you feel better,
I hope the rain
In your life,
Gets wetter.
I hope you two,
Are happy together,
It's goodbye to friends,
Friends forever…

DREAMING CASTLES

I've never built a sandcastle,
"What's the point?" I would say,
"The waves will come and wash it away."

I've never built a sandcastle
With its windows and a tiny door,
Maybe I have never dreamed before.

I've never built a sandcastle,
I feel forced to say
When you run up and ask me to play.

We walk down the beach hand in hand,
I watch you fill your red bucket,
With moistened sand.

I wonder how you know to pack it tight,
To tip it up,
And tap just right.

You take my hand now,
We search out a stick
And then run back to finish it quick!

When carving out the windows
And the tiny door,
I wonder why I never dreamed before.

HER TEDDY BEAR

I'm the teddy bear,
She has had since she was born,
I'm showing signs of aging now,
My fur matted and worn.

I'm her teddy bear,
She used to hold me at night,
I'm the one who knew instantly
When something wasn't right.

I'm her teddy bear,
I have watched her through the years,
I'm the one who's been there
To absorb her tears.

I'm her teddy bear,
You know I've seen her cry,
And it's me who listened
When she asked me why.

I'm her teddy bear,
I've seen her slam the doors,
There are days when she has come in cross,
And thrown me on the floor.

I'm her teddy bear,
She used to rub my ears,
I've been there when she's cried in pain
And was consumed by fear.

I'm her teddy bear,
You know, I witnessed their first kiss,
I'm so happy and proud of her,

She deserves moments like this.

I'll always be her teddy bear,
I still see her every day,
She's more smiles than tears now
And he makes her that way.

I'll always be her teddy bear,
Although it's him she holds at night,
Sometimes I do feel jealous
But I know it's only right.

I'll always be her teddy bear,
And now she is his wife,
I'm glad she has brought me along,
To watch over her new life...

MAKE UP IS FAKE

Make-up is fake,
I'm real,
Make-up says my face is easier to take,
But I'm real.

Why should I hide
A blemish or a scar,
Have they harmed me, so far?
Make-up is fake,
I'm real.

I've got a spot, I may wish wasn't there,
But it's not really me,
It's society that cares!
Make-up is fake,
But I'm real.

You say it gives confidence,
When you look good,
But who told you that you should?
Make-up is fake,
You're real.

Why does it matter,
That you haven't got perfect skin,
Because confidence, you know,
It comes from within.
Make-up is fake,
But you're real.

Yes, I have pride in my appearance, too,
I'm tidy and clean,
But I am me,

And I don't need to preen.
Make-up is fake,
I'm real.

Be yourself,
Your lipstick, is not what they'll remember,
Hold your head up,
Don't hide,
And never surrender,
Because
Make-up is fake,
But you're real.

HOMELESS

You do your best to avoid my eyes,
When you pass me every day,
You tell yourself
That there's no other way.

You walk on by,
Stare at your feet,
When you see me
Living on the street.

You try not to think
That I'm cold and lonely,
If only I was home with you,
If only...

You tell yourself
That you don't have the time,
Convince yourself I'm guilty
Of a crime.

You're on your way home
At night,
By train,
I wander,
Freezing,
Through darkness and rain.

Don't look at me blindly,
Please,
Don't avoid my eyes,
I know it's hard,
But listen to my cries.

Remember that I
Am a person too,
And remember that I,
Could easily be you.

THE OLD PIANO

There it stands
In the light
It sparkles,
As sunbeams spread
Like fingers,
Across the keys.
Soundless,
And waiting to be played.

The music
Resting there
On its stand,
A page of notes that dance.
There they stay
Frozen in time,
As they wait to be played.

There it stands
In the shadows
Now the sun has gone,
Large,
Dull,
Black,
It waits to be played.

BITTER... AND TWISTED

Today
I'm bitter
My body twists,
In pain.

Today
I'm angry,
My body
Fights my brain.

Today
I'm crying,
My body
Wins again.

Today
I'm worthless
And my body
Feels the same.

Today
I'm bitter,
And my body
Still remains.

CONFESSIONS OF A TEA JUNKIE

Alright, I did it!
Went shopping for teabags at midnight.
If I don't have one in the morning,
I don't feel right.

Forgot to buy the ones
I asked you for,
I was tempted to drain the one
Dropped on the floor!

Alright, I did it!
When we went out,
I wanted to know
If there was a kettle about!

After wandering for hours
I'd built up a thirst,
You didn't need to ask,
If it was tea or shops first!

Alright, I did it!
Deprived of my drug,
I thought about using one
Found in the plug!

You know it's been ages,
I am scratchy
And short,
Coming between me
And my tea,
Is a version of sport!

I know I'm terrible,

And I know it's tough,
But if I don't get the hot stuff,
I feel really rough!

I know you don't get it,
You can't understand,
Why I'm sitting here,
With shaking hands.

Now we have teabags
After nearly a day,
So Heaven help the person
Who gets in my way!

Some minutes later,
I'm holding my mug,
Gripping it tightly
Feels like a hug.

Pausing for a moment,
I breathe in the steam,
Those first blissful sips
Feel like a dream.

The result is instant,
Muscles relax,
My body is sealing,
And mending its cracks.

You can forget chocolate,
And forget a kiss,
I'm ashamed to admit
My paradise,
Is this!

DEAD

"She's dead,"
I said on the Sunday.
He asked me how I knew.
I answered
"Call it instinct,
You know,
I just do."

'You're dead'
I knew on the Sunday,
I hadn't kept anything down.
The Friday,
I had talked to you,
As I lay
On the ground.

I said,
"You know I love you,
I will do all I can"
Looking back now,
I think,
'It's two years on,
And I still don't understand'.

The scan
Happened on the Wednesday,
I was cold and sick.
'You're dead'
I thought as I lay there,
"No heartbeat"
Was what they said.

Tuesday,

They took you from me,
I was sound asleep.
'You're gone'
I thought when I woke up,
But our connection
Still runs deep.

I AM FREEDOM

I am freedom,
Your blissful release,
Search,
And discover,
The perfect peace.

I can't tell you,
How it feels to be free,
Search,
Yourself,
And live for me.

I know the struggle
You have to face,
Breathe,
A reprieve,
To find your space.

I am freedom,
Your distant dream,
Run,
With the sun,
In fields of green.

I know the battle,
You have to win,
Dance,
The chance,
You will find within.

I am a lover,
A gentle kiss,
A look,

All it took,
And you might have missed.

I can't tell you,
How it feels to be free,
Try,
Aim high,
And discover me.

A BAD SCENE

Reddened face
An angry fire,
I'm a saint,
And you're a liar!

Shattered glass
Where I took aim,
Lucky I missed,
But you're to blame!

Heated words
And broken hearts,
Ice cold silence,
We lie apart.

MUSIC OF THE NIGHT

She stands
In fading light,
Waiting for the peace of darkness
To wrap her in his arms.
The stars twinkle
Like glitter,
Her tiny specks of hope
In a blackening sky.

The breeze is gentle,
As he strokes her face.
The only sound is the leaves whispering.
Darkness brings her safety,
The warmth of his cloak.

The breeze,
With its dying breath,
Softly invites her in.
All is suddenly still,
To her pounding heart.

Silence,
He brings her comfort,
And speaks of mystery.
She smiles
And wipes her tears,
The day,
A world away.

TROUBLE IN PARADISE

Trouble in paradise,
Isolation,
Aggression
Slow falling rocks.

Rivers run dry,
No more feeling,
What's the point
In believing?

Trees stark naked,
Cold and exposed,
Like the emotions on our faces,
For the world to see.

Trouble in paradise,
Bereft of warmth and comfort,
No more colour or caring,
It leaves a barren land.

I WONDER

I wonder why it is so dark inside of me,
I wonder why I feel so cold.

The dream is fractured,
And pieces scattered,
All over the stone floor.

I wonder why I am so tired,
I wonder why you lied.

An empty room,
A chilling wind,
Blows through the window gap.

I wonder what I'll have left to show,
I wonder if you know.

A room once full of music,
Laughter and love,
Feels hollow now
And bare.

I wonder if I'll get back there,
I wonder if you care.

A space is left
Where our bed was,
An image of you and me.

As tears fall,
I stand alone
And memories are all I see.

Walking through the creaking door,
Out into the sun,
I can't do this,
I want to run.

I wonder now
As I turn the key,
Wonder what will become of me?

Life together lasted all those years,
And now,
Heartbroken,
It ends here.

GOING BACK

Where there were fields,
There are houses,
Crammed like sardines,
In a tin.

We would play,
Spend our days,
Running with the wind.

Those nights we watched for foxes,
Have been replaced by soulless boxes,
That people live within.

GONE WITH THE WIND

"Tomorrow is another day," Scarlett said.
But I disagree.
I think, you see,
The world will end now instead!

Because when he farts,
Things fall apart,
And I am totally gassed.
You have to help me,
Set me free,
From the thing that comes out his ass!

"Tomorrow is another day," Scarlett said.
But I disagree.
I hope, you see,
That the world will end now instead!

He's a champion farter,
I must be smarter,
And run right from the room,
Before the walls cave in,
At the demon within,
And I am sentenced to stinky doom!

"Tomorrow is another day," Scarlett said.
But I disagree.
I prey, you see,
The world will end now instead!

He says,
"Pull my finger!"
And the odour doth linger,
Forever and a day!

At that look on his face,
I must make haste,
And scram right out his way.

I love you Dad,
But you smell really bad,
And I wish you weren't my kin!
You are worse than the cat,
One more smell like that,
And I am
'Gone With the Wind!'

NO CHANGE, NO FUTURE

Don't you feel angry
At the state of the world?
We should feel ashamed
At the bloodshed.

Is it fair
That people starve,
Waste away,
Thin, neglected?

Don't you feel fury
At the mess in the world?
A mess that we
Created.

Is it right
That our planet is dying,
Choking, burning, frying?

Don't you feel nervous
At the time we are wasting,
Stalling, standing,
Watching?

We should scream,
Raise our voice,
We do have a choice,
Act now,
Or destroy ourselves.

MY REAL NAME IS SUSAN

My real name is Susan
But the Police don't know that.
For now, they know me as Jenny,
Who burgles, like a cat.

Online I am April
An expert in cyber-crime,
Collecting personal details,
They won't catch me, this time.

The bank thinks I'm Zoe,
A tall and leggy blonde.
I've emptied a neighbour's cheque account,
When they notice, I'll be gone.

On the plane, I will be Karen
Well dressed in business suit.
I'll be smart, rich and charming,
And drink champagne by the flute!

On beaches I'll be lying,
Still living for the con,
Behaving like I'm royalty,
And a beautiful sun kissed bronze.

They will catch me when I am old and grey,
When my life has hit the skids,
I'll be widowed by a rich man,
And have a couple of kids.

I am a lonely alcoholic
In a small house by the sea,
My real name is Susan,

But I've never found me.

TO HER

Rose petals floating on the breeze,
"To her"
They murmur solemnly,
Under rain and clouds of grey,
How life can change,
In a day.

She would have loved the people there,
Honoured by the fact they cared,
I look up a moment and think I see,
Her smiling figure
Under a tree.

She is dancing in fallen leaves,
Give me a moment to let me grieve,
Tears are running down their faces,
But I'll keep her memory
In the safest of places.

Her body is lowered into the ground,
Whispering wind the only sound,
I want to scream and need to cry,
But I can't ask questions
Or wonder why.

Hours later in the silence of home,
I sit on the stairs and ignore the phone,
Cradling only a cup of cold tea,
I'm lost in memories
Of her and me.

Twilight comes and the day is passed,
A streetlamp glows through the glass,

Slowly I climb the stairs to bed,
Lifting a hand
To my aching head.

When I'm lying down at last,
I think once more of the past,
In the moments before dreamless sleep,
"To her"
I whisper quietly.

OLD ENOUGH TO KNOW THE TRUTH

Cinderella and the prince
Got a divorce.
Happily ever after,
Not true of course!

Snow White, with her prince
That was way too tall,
Gave birth to children
That were rather small!

Cinders and Snow
Had nowhere to go,
Fairytale marriages fell apart.
So they took their stuff,
Wanted to shack up,
And disappeared by horse and cart!

Godmother, always happy
With her cheeks so pink,
Was made to enter rehab,
For the demon drink!

Wicked queens, evil witches,
All those fairytale bitches,
They too had to pay for their crimes.
Despite the magic,
Their downfall was tragic,
And now they're serving time!

Post 'true love's kiss,'
There was something amiss
In Sleeping Beauty's perfect life.
Her Prince met a gnome

And never came home,
Now he's free from the trouble
And strife!

Fairytales, you see,
They can never be,
All of which they seem.
You're long enough in the tooth
To be told the truth,
That you're better off
Keeping the dream!

SHIPWRECKED

My life is a shipwreck,
Drifting on uncontrollable sea.
Even the crew
Seem to desert,
Like rats do I suppose,
One by one.
The pieces of wood
That hold me together,
Have been pulled away.
The work,
And love,
And freedom
That were part of me,
Floats.
Then the waves begin to swallow them up,
The work and freedom at least.
I'll try not to disappear though,
And the love stays,
The living part of the shell.

BEDTIME TALE

The wolf ate Red Riding Hood
Then three pigs for his pud,
Sleeping Beauty's still asleep,
Little Bow Peep has found her sheep.

Cinderella's lost her shoe
Snow White still has work to do,
The wicked witches have turned nice,
The farmer's wife has kept the mice!

The pretty Rapunzel let down her hair,
But her Princie didn't care!
She was left up in her tower,
As Little Miss Muffet sat on a flower!
Humpty Dumpty fell off his wall,
Jack's Giant grew twice as tall!

Go to sleep now,
Snuggle down tight,
As I kiss your cheek,
And whisper,
Goodnight....

TORTURED SOULS

I am not alone,
He is with me
Always,
In my heart,
Mind,
And somewhat
Tormented soul.

I am not alone,
He is here
Always,
To hold me,
Care,
And be there.

I am never alone,
He comforts me,
Always,
In my darkest hours
And rescues
My
Tormented soul.

I am never alone,
He loves me
Always,
Protecting
And sheltering
A fevered,
Tormented soul.

We are not alone,
Together

We'll live and love,
Always,
And care,
For our
Tormented souls.

We are not alone,
Together
We share,
An irregular heartbeat,
Always,
A heart that breathes
As one,
To save
Our tormented souls.

We are never alone,
United,
We will share the warmth
Always,
And free
Our tormented souls.

GIVEN

Finding someone
To love you,
Isn't the easiest
Task.

After all
It's not something,
You can
Ask.

It has to be
Freely,
Given.

THE FOX AND ME

I feel like a fox,
Hunted
Hounded by government attack dogs.
I feel like unwanted vermin.
They make me feel worthless

There are too many of us,
'Scrounging', stealing from others,
Considered more worthy.
Soon the dogs will find me,
And tear me apart.

I am not a fox,
I am a person with a disability,
But now there's little difference,
Between a fox, and me.

WORDS CAN HURT

Before you make assumptions,
Think about how it feels,
Before you make assumptions,
Ask me what's real.

Before you accuse me,
Learn about the facts,
Before you accuse me,
Ask if you'd do that?

Before you judge me,
Put yourself in my place,
Before you judge me,
Say it to my face!

Before you slander me,
Open your mind and be alert,
Before you slander me,
Remember words can hurt.

BABY, UNFINISHED

I'm sorry baby for the life you did not live,
I'm sorry for the love that I can't give,
I'm sorry that you went before I knew you were there,
Don't think that mummy wouldn't have cared.

I really don't know why I'm writing to you now,
I guess the private me needs to come out
Somehow.
I'm sorry baby that you could not stay,
And because I flushed you away.

I'm sorry baby,
"Hello out there"
For the things I'll never get to share,
I'm sorry my baby and I'm letting you know,
Because there's nothing left to show.

I love you
Little baby,
And don't you forget,
These are days that mummy won't regret.

LUCKY

I'm lucky
Sitting here,
Cosy
And safe from the cold.
Lucky,
I have shelter
And a home.

I'm lucky
Sitting here,
Wondering what to eat for lunch,
Lucky,
I'm not a starving mass
Of dying skin
And bone.

I'm lucky
Sitting here,
Thinking of Christmas presents,
Lucky,
I don't face the season
Wandering
And alone.

I am lucky
Sitting here,
Family not far away
Lucky,
That I'm here at all,
And lucky,
I am loved.

THE FADED QUILT

Our love is like a faded quilt,
Comfortably warm,
It folds us in.

Its patchwork,
Our memories
Of blues,
Pinks
And grey.

Knitted together,
We are strong,
If in places,
A little frayed.

But,
I know
that if I died tomorrow,
I'd be happy
To live within it,
Forever.

FIRST LOVE

Somewhere in me,
Lies a past that we
Had to leave behind.

Talking to you again
Should be easier, but then,
We never said goodbye.

So this is closure
By a few weeks exposure,
To a person that was my first love.

Unanswered questions
And old suggestions,
I'm looking at from above.

That I'm happy now
Makes it easier somehow,
But you and I understand,
Wherever I will be
There's a piece of me,
That is always holding your hand.

WHILE YOU'RE AT THE SHOPS

Blank CD's please,
Pick up the spare house key,
A jar of Peanut Butter
And some stuff to clean the gutter!

Don't forget Tomato Sauce,
Or the Tea Bags, of course.
Dad says
Fetch his Chicken Pie,
And those screws he meant to buy!

While you're at it,
Writing Paper
(You can take it 'round to Granny later),
Could you pick up a TV mag?
And Dad says don't forget his fags!

While you're down there,
Put the lottery on,
This time don't get the numbers wrong!
Get some polish for Cindy's shoes,
Find a cure for Andy's flu.

Granny rang,
Don't forget her Gin,
Or Plastic Bags for the kitchen bin.

Thank you 'petal' - you're a good son.
Don't be late,
Love and kisses,
Mum.

ALL I CAN DO

I can't tell you
What you want to hear,
The meaning,
For me,
Will never be clear.

I can't tell you
What you want to know,
The reason,
To me,
Has yet to be shown.

I can't tell you
Why you cry,
So the answer,
For me,
Is not to try.

All I can do
Is just be here,
Let you
Vent your anger,
And shed your tears.

All I can do
Is hold you tight,
I'll stay
By your side,
Into the night.

All I can do
Is show you I care,
And tell you

That I,
Will always be there.

All I can do
Is just be your friend,
I'll wait
For that moment,
When your heart mends...

YOU WON'T WIN THIS TIME!

You won't win this time,
You can't hurt me,
Unlike before,
I'm strong now,
See?

You think you can break me,
That I won't cope,
You won't win this time,
I've got life,
And hope.

You think I will be there,
That I'll take the fall,
You won't win this time,
I won't answer your call.

You think you can beat me,
That's where you're wrong,
You won't win this time,
Been a doormat too long!

You thought you could ask me,
I couldn't say no,
You didn't win this time,
I told you
Where to go!

POOR SANTA!

Poor Santa had clumsy feet,
For every time he had to repeat
This sliding down the chimney lark
He tripped and stumbled in the dark!

Poor Santa had a tickly nose
And with so many places left to go,
He'd fallen once again to his sooty knees
As he held back yet another sneeze!

Poor Santa decided it was worth a try
For another bite of a fresh mince pie
And when reaching upwards for the plate,
Clumsily fell over some roller skates!

Poor Santa he hurtled towards the door
The pesky plate shattering to the floor,
Next there came his loud 'Hic Choo',
And Santa didn't know what to do!

Poor Santa had made so much noise
He woke up the little girls and boys,
Tiny feet padding down the stairs
He knew that they would catch him there.

Poor Santa this night, so far it was tragic.
At the last moment he remembered his magic,
With a click of his fingers and seconds to spare,
He luckily vanished into the air!

Poor Santa red faced and out of breath,
One year those children would be his death,
Slowly he clambered in to his sleigh,

Relived to make a clean get away!

As he took to the air with a 'Ho Ho Ho'
There was something poor Santa didn't know,
Those startled children were aghast to find
He'd gone and left his full sack behind!

GOODBYE TO ALL THAT

Goodbye to all that,
Don't think I care,
For lost days and endless hours,
You left me standing there.

Goodbye to all that,
A lifetime's anger, buried pain,
Now I've learnt my lesson,
I won't go there again.

Goodbye to all that,
You can tell me I'm a quitter,
But I won't let your actions
Ever make me bitter.

Goodbye to all that,
You said you'd be there, but you weren't,
Don't think I ever trusted you,
Once my fingers got burnt.

Goodbye to all that,
They say 'blood, it's thicker than water,'
You forgot that I'm a person,
Not a lamb for slaughter.

Goodbye to all that,
I think now you'll find,
I won't let you take up the space
You once did, within my mind.

Goodbye to all that
Your words can't get to me,
Where once I had my demons,

I've learnt to set them free.

Goodbye to all that,
It was a battle that I've won,
Because now I've got the strength to say,
I've had enough - I'm done!

MY THOUGHTS ARE LONELY

My thoughts are lonely
Desperation claws
A lifetime's memories
Drench the floor.

My thoughts are lonely
In my darkened room
Trapped inside
Never fading
Doom.

My thoughts are lonely
Now they scream
Reflected images
A frozen dream.

My thoughts are frightened
Muscles tense
They plea for a moment
Of common sense.

My thoughts are frightened
As I lie alone
The fear grips
And chills my bones.

My thoughts now calmer
The panic is past
The slow release
Of the shadows cast.

My thoughts are calmer
The sun peeps through

Fear is broken
Life's anew.

SIMPLICITY

I don't need jewellery or a flashy car
I need things that are more befitting of me,
I need endless paper and pens,
With cups of steaming tea.

My wedding ring is a plain silver band,
No diamonds or flashy brightness,
For as long as I can hold your hand,
I will bask in its rightness.

I don't want lots of money or the latest thing,
I just want time to read my books,
And a space
Where I can sing.

I don't need craziness and chaos
Or a life of screaming kids,
I am happy when the sun goes down,
And we are all there is.

Our house isn't massive,
It doesn't have to be pristine,
It's cosy and loved and you are there,
So I am living my dream.

SOMETIMES

Sometimes,
There are life changing moments,
Someone turns on the light,
And all the darkness disappears,
Everything is clear,
Like when the world
Brought me,
To you.

Sometimes,
When you stop struggling
Against the violent tide,
It will take you
Closer,
To where you need to be.

You will walk upon
Warm sand again,
And feel the blazing sun,
Just like I did,
On that day
The world brought me,
To you.

WHEN YOU ARE NOT WITH ME

When you are not with me
I fall apart,
Every second
Breaks my heart.

When you are not with me
There's an empty space,
I don't feel part
Of the human race.

When you are not with me
Hours expand,
Wish I could be there
To hold your hand.

When you are not with me
I fade away,
Minutes drag
Into wasted days.

When you're not with me
Silence is my friend,
I wait patiently
For the day to end.

Now you are with me
You walk through the door,
I forget all
That went before.

Now you are with me
Back home at last,
My lonely day

For now in the past.

Now you are with me
My heart beats faster,
Like a puppy reunited
With its master.
Now you are with me
Anxiety calms,
I feel safe
When I'm back in your arms.

Now you are with me
My spirits are high,
Now we are together
Hours will fly.

MY WORDS

Today my words are empty,
They stand like used milk bottles,
Vacant and neglected,
Fragile, unprotected.

They once shimmered in sunlight,
Waiting on the doorstep
Until I ask them in.
Now they're left for another day,
Because no one lives within.

Today the skies have darkened,
A heavy leaden grey,
My words
That once were lively,
Have softly slipped away.

Tomorrow a gust of wind may blow,
I might hear a shattering sound,
Those perfect shimmering milk bottles
Will lie in pieces
On the ground.

FINDING INSPIRATION

I'm not having much luck today
Finding inspiration.
I look,
Maybe as many others do,
At the stars before dawn,
And hope,
That they will shine light
Into my darkness.

I'm not having much luck today
Finding inspiration.
My first taste of tea,
That would bring me warmth
and comfort,
Instantly clearing
My clouded mind,
Stands untouched,
And cold.

I'm not having much luck today,
Finding inspiration.
The sun,
That dances across my table top,
Making me smile,
Has disappeared,
Seemingly forever,
Behind its cloud.

I'm not having much luck today,
Finding inspiration.
The music,
That plays in my mind
And on the stereo,

Is empty,
The notes feel silent,
And words mean nothing.

I haven't had much luck today
Finding inspiration.
The breeze of life,
That picks me up
And helps me to fly,
Has gone,
And not taken me with it.
My world is still.

WRITE AGAIN

She's back
And she says she's OK,
No more obstacles
Stand in her way,
She can even write again.

I'm back
And I tell them what they want to hear,
While inside I drown
In unshed tears,
I've told them I can write again.

She's back
And she is feeling fine,
She just needed
A little time,
We're relieved that she can write again.

I'm back
And I told them all is well,
But they don't know
How far I fell,
I wish that I could write again.

She's back you know
And she is strong,
About time we feel,
It's been so long,
We're happy she can write again.

I'm back
And I confess
I have been lying,

Because you wouldn't want to see me crying,
Though I know I'm nearly right again.

She's back
We thought she was before,
But she cried
When she closed the door,
We hope she can feel alright again.

I'm back you know
I'm on top form,
I've fought the battle,
Braved the storm,
And now I can really write again.

MR FOX

Mr Fox is on the prowl again
He's been rooting through the neighbour's bins
To find himself a tasty treat,
A juicy morsel he can eat,
Tomorrow morning to her rage,
It's regurgitated over the page.

Mr Fox I see his eyes are bright,
He wonders what he'll find tonight,
In daylight he will hide his mirth,
'Til he finds out what a picture's worth.

But the stars you know, they question why
Mr Fox and Co will cheat and lie,
For years it seems their phones were hacked,
They were angry when the fox attacked.

For fame and wealth anonymity was traded,
Now they're shocked to find their lives invaded,
Mr Fox you see he'll always win,
While the public feed on celebrities' sin

THE MAN IN THE MOON

I watch from the warmth
Of my bed,
His light bathes my face,
And I know I can never
Touch him.

Sometimes he seems
Close to me,
And lives
In the perfect ball.

Other times
He turns his light away,
Or softly changes
Shape.

He watches over me
In slumber,
A beautiful
Protective glow.

In dreams I am with him,
We exist side by side,
And I am his comfort,
Just as he
Is mine.

As the sun rises,
He kisses my cheek,
Whispering gently,

"Wake my love,
And I'll return

Tonight."

A FACELESS BOOK

I don't want
To be your friend,
I don't know you now
And didn't want to then!

 Forgive me
Ignoring your friend requests
But I won't invite
Unwanted guests!

You'll get this note now
And sorry if it's late,
But do you really care
About my status update?

So go away,
Live your life, do whatever
But don't flaunt it at me
Like it's something clever!

Congratulations, hooray,
You got married, had kids,
But would you really care,
If my life hit the skids?

To those I love
Who are on my list,
You know me better,
Forget all this.

To those that don't
Who are really pissed,
I will bend over,

And you can kiss this!

WHAT MATTERS

I see sunshine
Where there once was rain,
Feel happiness,
Where there once was pain.

It doesn't matter which box
They put me in,
What really matters,
Is what's within.

HAPPY

I feel so happy today
For now there is no pain,
I am floating high above cloud nine
And dancing in the rain.

I feel so happy today
There is sunlight on my face,
All that agony that was there before
Has left without a trace.

I feel so happy today
You won't take that away,
I'll be standing for as long as I can
And begging it to stay.

I feel so happy today
A perfect peace descends.
I'll grasp it for as long as I can
And hold it 'til the end.

I feel so happy today
I will again tomorrow,
And for all the days after that
I'm done with pain and sorrow.

I feel so happy today
Here's to defying gravity,
The world can take another shot
It will never destroy me.

ANXIETY

I can't breathe
Anxiety
I can't see ahead of me
I can't stand it
That you took my self-esteem
And I dream
I'll get it back.

I can't sleep
Panic
And I'm frantic
About independence lost
So I'll fight
Whatever the cost.

I can't move
Stress
As you try
To repress
Our voices,
How can I,
When you take our choices?

THE GIRL IN BLUE

The girl in blue stood in a foggy haze,
Not realising she'd wandered,
On to a railway.

Christmas Eve,
Nineteen thirty three,
Would be the last one.
She'd ever see.

The night time closed in,
And the fog, thickened,
She knew not,
Where she was,
And her heartbeat, quickened.

Reaching out a hand,
To the icy air
A thunderous roar,
Said she shouldn't be there.

She tried to move,
But frozen with fright,
The last thing she saw,
Was the brightest light...

PLEASE UNDERSTAND

Sometimes I want to scream that you betrayed me,
You said that we would face this together
Through even then
I knew it wouldn't last forever.

Despite your words I somehow knew
That you would become a mother,
And I can think of no other friend
I would want it for more.

But it breaks my heart that your choices
Will never be mine,
I feel like I've committed a crime
Because I can't share your joy,

Telling myself I'm glad you're happy
And that I need more
Than changing nappies,
Is really no comfort at all.

I miss you,
I miss the way we used to be,
I miss caring and sharing,
And knowing you were there for me.

I don't want this pain, this deep gnawing ache,
And I think to myself
'Oh for God sake, can't you just snap out of it?'
But I know it isn't that easy
And I hate the bitterness,
It isn't me.

I fear what I've become.

I want to be there when you're tired
And listen when you're stressed,
But feel resentment that I can't express,
'Yeah well, it's alright for some!'

I know that this is hard for you too,
And I don't know what to do
When I feel the gaps get wider.

As more friends becpme mother's,
Another and another,
My world is filled with prams and baby scans,
I'm starting to feel smothered.

And once again you know,
I want to scream,
Because you
Are living my dream.

At the same time you shouldn't feel bad,
Or guilty about the luck you've had,
Be proud and happy, and free,
The only one that can deal with this
Is me.

I love you
And I am proud of you,
I love that you are doing it all
Just as I would do.

I wrote this down to work through my issues
Like you've always said I should,
Apologies though, if you're needing tissues,
I always knew you would!

I guess it's all about hearing now,
I don't know when I'll be done,
There are good days
And then so desperately sad,
But keep thinking about the fun we've had,
And all we used to do.

I want caring, sharing
And feel glad,
And I need a friend
Like you...

A HOME FOR FRED

It was so quiet
The old shepherd's hut on the moor,
Always in darkness
With dust on the floor.

A rusted kettle,
A blanketed bed,
Even in winter,
A home for Fred.

There was a small fire
On which he could bake,
But on stormy nights,
The roof would shake!

He meant to fix holes
Through which came the rain,
But he couldn't climb the ladder,
Far too much pain.

Once he'd had a job
And he'd painted the walls,
Now they were rotting
And soon they would fall.

Don't think Fred is lonely,
He has his sheep,
At nightfall their noises,
Will lull him to sleep.

In summer the sun shines
Through broken windows,
And where Fred will wander,

Nobody knows!

But he'll always come back,
For it is nature he loves,
The changing of the seasons,
And the wide skies above.

THEY CUT, WE BLEED

Disabled people,
dying and desperate
We are scared,
At government hands!

For our lives,
We shout,
Please understand
What this is really about.

Independence taken,
We're shaken,
By an envelope
On the mat.

'It's the cost', they say,
Benefits lost,
Because you're just,
Not worth that!

I would give anything
To be free from disability,
'Scrounger rhetoric'
Kills a piece of me.

Confidence gone,
And fear in place
Each one of us, has a name, a face.

We are begging
And pleading.
Because when they cut,
We are bleeding!

THEY WILL FALL

They will fall, one by one,
Like leaves from trees,
They will get what they want,
And then scuttle away,
Because there is no longer
A reason to stay.

It will be us, still here,
Year after year,
Maybe we are the trees?
Always rooted and never free.

The leaves, they never ask us,
What we feel, or what we've seen?
Only concerned with what
They have been!

They will fall,
Like leaves from trees,
Used, brown and crisp,
Deciding they have nothing
Left to give, or gain,
And when the leaves drift off,
The trees, remain.

MOMENTS OF MAGIC

I search for moments of magic
You find in every day,
I hope that they will take away
The pain.

I watch the sun reflecting
On a table top,
Like fairies dancing in a circle,
Smile at the thought.

I search for moments of magic
To brighten up my day
I hope that they
Will last a while,
And take away the pain.

I hold tight to a mug,
The warmth refreshes me.
A single second of perfect bliss,
Like softness
Of a kiss.

QUEEN OF NEW YORK CITY

I was supposed to be Queen,
Now I work in a coffee shop,
I add extra sugar and put sprinkles on top!
They threw me out,
I was not what I was meant to be,
I called for abolition of the monarchy!
They wanted someone to wear gowns with a tiara
But I'm more flannelette Pyjamas
And smudged mascara!
I don't want round the world trips
Just to smile and shake hands
I'll take unplanned road trips in the back of a van.
They wanted someone quiet and apolitical
Turning up to make speeches
Thoughtless, hypocritical!
I'd have to marry elite, Keep the bloodline pure,
Forget 'who brought me home?'
I can't be sure!
I don't want to be a rich bitch
I would always say things I shouldn't,
So I'd rather give up the throne, than be something I couldn't!

TEA BAGS AND CRICKET BATS

She noticed she wasn't in pain today
And wondered why?
Had she died overnight?
Something wasn't right.
Reality skewed
And time...confused.
Maybe she had run out of teabags!
Raise red flags
Until you find a box
Pick locks if you have to-
Do whatever you must do!
She's making rhymes
Out of nothing again,
And because she's depends
On her watery drug
She's forgotten there's a spider
Tucked under the rug!
Hubby, impressed
she's not squealing like a girl,
Remains unaware
That her toes are curled,
And if he doesn't do something
To remedy that,
She may well hit him
With a cricket bat!

HOLD MY HAND

I've already tried walking away,
I'm too tired
I don't care today.

I've already tried to say no,
Go away,
Just leave me alone.

I've already tried to lose the guilt
Fake a smile
Make up for the tears spilt.

I've already tried to get some sleep
Curled up in a ball,
Anxieties creep.

I've already tried to forget sorrow
For better days
I'll beg, steal, borrow.

I've already tried being strong
But it's killing me inside
And the days are too long.

I've already tried all that you say
You expect so much
That I've pushed you away.

Why don't you try to understand?
Words aren't needed now
Just hold my hand.

SHADOWS

I live in shadows
You only see me,
As light shines, randomly.
In darkness deep
A dreamless sleep
So you decide, what's real?

SECTION TWO

THE SHORT STORIES

SINGING FOR ST PETER

"Are you new here?" She asked him, as he floated up to sit beside her. Usually Rowena would object to sharing her cloud, but he was still looking a bit lost so she took pity on him.

"I arrived yesterday. I'm Scott." He extended his hand to shake hers.

"Rowena," she replied simply, shaking his hand. "...and you didn't get your wings yesterday, did you?"

"No I didn't...but until earlier, I just figured it was something like 'It's a Wonderful Life.'"

"Oh, please...!" she replied, laughing. "You don't really believe all that rubbish, do you? It's just a story! Things are a lot simpler than that..."

"I know that now, but I didn't know what to believe. It all happened so fast. This time yesterday, I was having a picnic in the woods with my family, and I got stung by a bee. The next thing I know, I'm singing for St Peter, over there!"

Rowena made a face and suppressed the urge to laugh again,

"Oh, I know! We ALL heard you! ...You do realise, that you're completely tone deaf, don't you?"

"I do now! Scott grimaced at the memory, "Anyway, I just thought it was a myth, that all angels could sing and that it really wouldn't matter."

"Yes, well..." she replied, smiling at him, "It is a myth... in your case!"

He stuck his tongue out at her in response. Maybe this death lark wouldn't be so bad after all. He may have made a new friend.

"When I got here, some people in the queue at the pearly gates were asked to sing too, and they were given their wings, straight away."

She shifted uneasily and stared at the space where the floor should be.

"Yes, but they sounded better than you though, didn't they?"

"Oh yeah; they sounded, positively...angelic!" he smirked and looked at her.

"Ha, ha, very funny! What did Peter say, when you sang at him?"

Now it was his term to laugh, as he remembered, St Peter's reaction.

"He was totally deadpan, then he told me to "go, and bother Satan!"

She knew it was unusual for Peter to be so harsh, but it was funny and to be honest, she wasn't surprised! Scott's voice was worse than she had ever heard before.

"Then what happened?" Rowena was almost afraid to ask, but this could be the best entertainment she'd had all week!

Scott looked ashamed, and cleared his throat, "It's was all rather awkward...I sang for Satan too, and he sent me back here!"

It was all she could do, not to fall off the cloud, through laughing so much! Knowing it was wrong to laugh at someone else's misfortune just made it worse! Satan sending someone back was unheard of!

After a while, she regained her composure.

"I'm sorry. It's not funny...but anyway, you're here, so...what did Peter say, when you came back up? I bet it wasn't very saintly!"

"It wasn't! He swore at me and told me that no amount of singing lessons were going to help me, but that I had to get my wings somehow. They couldn't have people sitting around on clouds, doing nothing. This wasn't a holiday camp; there had to be rules, even in heaven!"

"I see"

"Yes... so then he disappeared off, and came back later with some boxes. I thought he was packing me off somewhere, so I got quite anxious, until he opened the box and gave me a can... several cans, actually!"

Rowena frowned. She didn't think getting sloshed was the answer to this particular problem! Peter obviously hadn't heard drunken people sing karaoke! This man's voice was bad enough when he was sober!

"Cans; Of what?!"

"I know," Scott replied, "Peter said, 'You're beyond help, my lad. You'd better drink this, and lots of it! It's 'Red Bull'...It gives you wings!"

FOR JOYCE

I found the story of Joyce Carol Vincent very disturbing since I first heard about it a couple of years ago.

She was a young woman who lay dead in her London flat for three years. Her family lost touch with her and having resigned from her job, she detached herself from friends.

I still feel really uneasy when I think about it, and I think it says a lot about how (in today's society) people can get lost whether they intend to or not.

They live a life of isolation and loneliness.

Loneliness is increasingly becoming a problem, with families spread out and cuts to the services which enable people to get out and about.

Eventually, researchers managed to piece Joyce's life together and the film 'Dreams of a Life' was made.

I gradually managed to put Joyce's story to the back of my mind. That is until recently, when somebody mentioned the film to me.

The reason I'm writing this is to say that if there's someone you haven't spoken to for a while and you miss them, pick up the phone, or pop in, because for someone like Joyce it could have made all the difference.

THE AMBASSADOR HOTEL, LOS ANGELES – A LANDMARK LOST

I want to tell you about the much loved, (and much missed), 'Ambassador Hotel' in Los Angeles.

I began researching the hotel after I read about it in the mid 1990's. To me, it was, (and still is), fascinating on many levels.

Not only was it an abandoned, decaying building with unique and beautiful features, but it held so much history; so much mystery, glamour, drama, and ghosts from an era that was long gone.

My imagination was set on fire by the place.

The hotel opened in December 1929. It became popular with many of the Hollywood stars of the 'golden age.' Anyone who was anyone in L.A at that time stayed there - from Presidents to actors, writers to artists. They stayed there, lived there, partied, romanced, - and died there.

The first Oscar ceremony took place in the ballroom, as did many afterwards. Many Hollywood movies were filmed within its walls too, including *The Graduate*.

Marilyn Monroe got her first modelling job there, when she was simply Norma Jean Baker. Frank Sinatra, Judy Garland and Barbra Streisand were just a few of the greats who performed at the world famous *Coconut Grove nightclub*, situated within the hotel.

Much later, in June 1968, it was in the pantry of this hotel that Robert Fitzgerald Kennedy was assassinated. After those tragic events, the hotel struggled. This was compounded by a sharp decline in the surrounding neighbourhood.

The hotel, with its beautiful art deco features, staircases, and ever-present echoes of Hollywood's history, finally closed its doors at the end of 1989.

Between then and its demolition, it continued to be used as a filming location. In fact, the last thing to be filmed there was *Bobby* - a film about the lives of (fictionalised) hotel staff, and Robert Kennedy's last campaign. The hotel was already being demolished as the last scenes were shot.

I wish it was still standing, and I wish I could've gone there, to soak up the atmosphere and explore the halls. As with many places, it was so much more than just a building, and it should have been treasured and looked after.

History is valuable and I think sometimes, when money is involved, it is easy to forget that. By the time you've remembered, it's often too late.

AN ENDURING PASSION FOR A CAUSE

Is it hard, being a campaigner?

It was easier, when I was younger - before this government. Before this government, it was access issues: "Excuse me, any chance we could have a ramp here?"; "These doors could be electric, you know...?"; "Yes, but when you get the wheelchairs INSIDE the lift, there's barely any room to close the door!" or, "Excuse me, you can't do that, these buses need level access. You're breaking the law...!"

Now, it's "but they're killing us! People are starving..."

It's being told we're any variant of 'benefit scrounging scum' on an almost daily basis, by this government, or the media. I've lost count of the times I've had to say, "Actually, those figures aren't correct. You're being lied to. Benefit fraud is actually...percent!'

I feel worthless every time the government spouts more 'scrounger rhetoric' and lies to people. I'm not a 'scrounger' - I'm Helen- and for the record, disabled, and ill people have to struggle just to manage the easiest of tasks and just to get through the day! Surely, that is the very definition of 'striving?!' But no, that doesn't count! WE don't count, now.

Even when I'm trying to 'take a break,' my brain won't switch off. There's guilt. I feel like I should be doing this, that, or the other. I should be reading or writing this, that or the other, even though I'm not well enough.

I'm getting better at saying, (to myself), I'll do it later. But it still takes ages for the knots to leave my stomach.

I'm not alone. There are so many of us that carry those feelings around with us, and the fight never stops! If we don't make a stand and say that all this anxiety, fear, suffering, pain, and death, is wrong, - who will?!

We can't count on the law to protect us, because the government will change that if something doesn't go their way!

We can't count on many politicians to protect us because they are the problem! As is their harmful and twisted ideology - which says the poor and vulnerable should suffer, while the rich pay less tax, get bonuses, and kick us while we're down!

Nobody asks for a disability or illness. It's not a choice! Nobody asks to be poor, either. We are fighting harder now and it's a different fight to when I started. We have to fight for basics, and the right to be viewed as human beings rather than nameless 'scroungers!'

I never thought this could, or would happen; but it is, and we're living it.

Is it hard, being a campaigner? It's beyond hard, and it's heartbreaking.

I wouldn't wish what so many people are going through on my worst enemy, and I often feel that whatever I do, it is never enough.

I won't get started on 'group politics,' self-imposed campaigner hierarchies, egos, and the day-to-day grind of the way it all works! That's another layer of stress!

That's why I stay out of groups and I don't have any party allegiances. I speak for myself, and myself only. If people agree with me, fine. If people don't, that's fine, too!

The cause is more important than me. It's more important than any one person. I believe in it with everything that I am. And even though I want to run away screaming on a regular basis, and never campaign another day in my life. I can't do that. It's part of me. It always has been - and it always will be.

THE LAST DAY

The last person to turn out the lights was a security guard.

After twenty five years protecting this building, its staff and patients, he had come to love the way the old staircases sounded when he stepped on them, knowing where to put his feet to make each floorboard creak.

He had taken note of every patient as they entered through the heavy front door and passed in the lobby. He'd seen the confusion and fear and confusion in their eyes, and heard every cry.

He waited for the day when they left, confident and well enough to return to life in the 'real world'. They would shake hands and hug him to say 'goodbye.' He would reply that he hoped not to see them again! With a smile and eagerness of step, they would leave through the heavy front door.

There were some that never left of course. Bob lost count of the poor souls he had had to cut down from a ceiling beam or light fitting – and the bodies he had escorted down in the rickety old lift to take up their space in the mortuary.

Bob recognised all of them, and each death left a pain somewhere in his heart. Over time he felt he knew which people would end their days at Blackheath. They had a more quiet confusion and when he looked into those eyes and took hold of those hands, he saw a more profound sense of loss – like something inside them had given up.

Sometimes Bob got it wrong, and he was pleased to help carry the belongings of a 'recovered' person to a waiting taxi, or watch as they were embraced by a grateful loved one. Nothing made him happier than when he got it wrong. He always hoped he would.

The best part of Bob's job was the people - the patients, the cleaning staff, the doctors and nurses with whom he had shared many an hour of banter. Those people had become his friends, and the beautiful building was much more than just a workplace now. It was a second home. He knew every inch of it, from which door had the trickiest lock to which piece of the old pipe work had last sprung a leak!

Nobody ever really stuck to their given jobs. Where it was possible, they all just sort of mucked in. They were more than friends, they were a family, and as he ran his hands over the wooden panelling of the last door he locked, Bob had tears in his eyes.

THE RIGHT WAY

"Not that right, - the right, right!" The instructor said, as I turned left.

"You should hold your hands up..." my mother would say. "The one that makes an L..."But that's not advisable when your hands are on the steering wheel! I don't think writing 'L' and 'R' on my thumbs was a wise move for my first driving lesson either. The instructor visibly paled as I got into the driver's seat and he caught me double checking them! What's even more worrying is that all these months later, they still need to be there, only now I have to paint my nails too – just to be sure! Black for the left hand and red for the right...or was it the other way 'round?

You know, it's funny. All those months ago, my instructor didn't get very thirsty at all during our lessons. Now he carries a small black flask which he drinks from regularly. Although granted, his swigs are bigger after I've done the roundabout in the centre of town.

Lately, as I know how thirsty he gets, I've started bringing cans of Coke for him. I like to be helpful, and there's nothing worse than being thirsty is there? When I told him that, he muttered a swear word – or several!

Anyway, I think I'm improving a bit. Now I've worked out that if I go in the opposite direction to what he says, then I'll be going the right way. It seems to work, well, so far anyway! I wonder if he's booked my test yet?

LOST AND FOUND

April 1995.

"Please don't make me give it up" I said, slowly kneeling to get from the floor to the sofa.

My physio sighed and looked over at me. "I know how much you love it", she replied, "but it's not good for you..."

It was my turn to sigh. "Can't I just have one more year? I've hardly started..."

"If you have one more year, your hips will be worse. You've already said you're struggling with the pedal...'

"But I've just bought myself some proper sticks and brushes..."

"I know" she replied, putting her arm around me, "but your hips and your knees will suffer, and I wouldn't be a very good physio if I let you carry on, would I?" I bit my lip in an attempt to stop myself from crying - and failed!

"No...I know"

She handed me a tissue from a small packet in her handbag,

"I'm sorry..."

"It's not your fault" I said, as sobs, became hiccups.

"I just don't like having to stop you doing something that means so much to you...Will you need a letter for your teacher?"

"Probably", I muttered quietly, and hiccupped again.

It was a foggy Thursday morning when I left my maths lesson and made the short journey in my wheelchair across lower school playground to the dusty old porta-cabin.

I got out of my chair, and struggled up the few wooden steps, in exactly the same way I had almost every Thursday morning for just over a year.

I swallowed, as I knocked lightly on the door, and a knot formed in my stomach.

"Come on in, Helen" Mr Claymore said, in the same slightly brusque way he always did.

"Hello", he smiled, and came over to help me get to the stool, "have you got your sticks?"

"No..." I replied, so quietly that I could barely hear myself speak. I cleared my throat, "I'm sorry. I came to tell you that I can't play the drums any more. I have to stop my lessons."

Mr Claymore leant against the desk, "You were doing so well..." he told me sadly.

I smiled, although by this time, I had tears in my eyes.

"I wasn't. I was struggling with the pedals. My knees hurt, and my physio says I need to stop, but I really don't want to. I'm sorry...."

"Ah...I understand, but I'll be sorry to see you go..."

"Maybe after surgery I can come back..." I replied hopefully, -even though I knew it wasn't realistic.

"I hope so", he replied, but I think he knew what I did - it wasn't really going to be possible.

He helped me down the stairs of the dusty porta-cabin and I cried as I sat in my wheelchair. I wanted to play the drums so badly, and it had become another thing I couldn't do.

Mr Claymore didn't see me cry, but as I began to push myself across the playground, he called out to me.

"Helen - you can sing! You love that, so do that instead. Take lessons - use what you already have! No one can take that from you'!

By the time I got back in, and down the corridor to my maths lesson, I was smiling again.

CHRISTMAS IS OFF!

Rudolph opened a sleepy eye and surveyed the scene. There was no fresh hay, and no one had brought his breakfast yet! It was definitely that time of year again. Hic choo! Yes, definitely that time of year again, for Rudolph had a cold. It would help of course, if there was fresh hay and a bit of breakfast when it was required. Neglect, that's what this was – someone should call the RSPCA!

Rudolph tapped on the ground impatiently with a hairy hoof, and waited. Prancer jerked awake at the sound. Sharing a stall with a diva had its drawbacks! Prancer peered at his companion and noticed that, once again, his nose was red, swollen and sore. Prancer tried to suppress the silent joy that welled up in him. After all, it wasn't charitable to take pleasure in someone else's misfortune, even if it was Rudolph's! Instead, he said brightly, "Gee Rudy, you have a cold!"

His words were greeted by a disdainful huff and a gruff, "State the bloomin'...hic choo...obvious, why don't you?!"

Prancer smiled inwardly, and closed his eyes again.

Just over an hour later, Norm, the bespectacled elf appeared, "Sorry I'm late boys! Been a bit hectic upstairs..."

Rudolph said nothing, but noted the elf's change in clothing. The usual comfortable brown over shirt had been replaced by a green and red apron. On it were embroidered the words *The North Pole welcomes the Festive Season.*

"Festive, my arse!" Rudolph muttered, and began to munch his hay.

Just then, Mrs Claus appeared in the doorway with her hands on her hips. Her face was pinker than usual. Norm wandered over to her and draped his arm around her shoulders. The reindeers exchanged glances, 'Aye, aye, what's going on here then?' From the doorway they clearly heard the words "Christmas is OFF!"

Much later, the reindeers were still in shock. Rumours, whispers and speculation suddenly abound. Had the placid, loving, long-suffering Mary Claus finally had enough of her husband? Was she going to leave the North Pole with a certain bespectacled elf?

"Let's face it," Rudolph interjected between sneezes, "he's Brad Pitt by comparison!" The other reindeers sniggered, but no one could avoid the dark clouds of doom that seemed to be gathering over the North Pole.

It was just before dawn the next day, when a large man wearing faded jeans and a crumpled shirt that was two sizes too small wandered aimlessly into the stalls. Rudolph failed to recognise him at first, but as he came closer, the long white beard gave him away. A beard which contained pieces of cornflake, traces of tomato sauce and if Rudolph wasn't mistaken, chocolate cake.

"So this is what Santa Claus looks like on his days off is it?" Rudolph mused, "Charming!"

Santa pulled up a stool and perched beside Norm, who, for most of the night, had been sitting reading a novel. Rudolph watched. There may well be fisticuffs. What would happen then?! The two men sat in silence for a while. It was Santa who spoke first, eventually.

"I'm too big for the sleigh" he said simply.

"I know," Norm responded, putting his book down, "she did warn you, Claus. She tried to change your diet, bought you one of those 'Wii' thingies to help you exercise more. She knows how much you love your 'Playstation.'

"Yes", came the soft reply.

Rudolph listened to the anguished conversation. A moment ago, he had nudged Prancer awake and now they stood alert, uncertain and hardly daring to breathe.

It was true that Rudolph hated Christmas. He hated the chaos, the long, seemingly endless journey and his constant...hic choo...colds, even if they had helped make him famous. But he loved Claus. They all did. Rudolph caught

Prancer's eye, and they knew they had to do something. For now though, captive audience that they were, they carried on listening.

"You kept on eating, sneaking food when you thought no one was looking," Norm was saying matter-of-factly, "and that 'Wii' thing is still in its box!" Santa nodded sadly. "There must be another way..." Santa said quietly, "We can't just cancel Christmas. Think of the children!"

Despair crossed his features as he thought of all the children around the world that he would let down. "Someone could go in your place." Norm said brightly, trying to sound hopeful, but he knew what Santa's response would be, and he was right. "It's against the rules!" Santa replied, his voice gruff with emotion. Norm stared at the floor and thought for a moment. Suddenly, an idea struck him. A magnificent idea!

"We could make the sleigh BIGGER!" Norm exclaimed excitedly.

The little elf began hopping from foot to foot as enthusiasm took hold of him, and his imagination ran riot. Santa looked over at his friend, "We could, but there is just not enough time Norm!" Santa sounded helpless. "We have just over a week," Norm replied, shaking Claus by the shirt in excitement. "IT CAN BE DONE!"

While the workshop hustled and bustled, hammered and sawed, the reindeers went into conference themselves.

"I see we weren't consulted about any of this!" Dancer commented, between bites of carrot.

All the other reindeers turned to him. "SHUT UP!" they cried in unison.

"Was only saying,'" Dancer muttered.

"Well, don't!" Rudolph replied, hammering a hoof on the ground with authority.

"Hey man, you had a visit from the ghosts of past, present and future or something?!" Dancer questioned, tilting his head to one side "You hate Christmas!"

Rudolph was ruffled, "I hate...hic...choo...Christmas, but I don't hate Claus!"

There was silence for a moment while the other reindeers looked at Rudolph with new eyes. Maybe he wasn't as selfish and egotistical as they all thought he was. Perhaps they had judged him unfairly." We need to contact 'The Reindeer Council'"... Prancer spoke up ... "There won't be enough of us to pull the... uh, new sleigh." "Consider it done!" Donner called from the back stall. The reindeers, a short time ago filled with such uncertainty, now found themselves bursting with a new sense of optimism and camaraderie.

As dusk descended on Christmas Eve, the Pole was alive

and buzzing like never before. In the workshop dishevelled looking elves, led by an ecstatic Norm, tested and retested the extended sleigh. Its front had been widened and painted beautifully with gold, red and black paint. The pieces of metal that held the contraption together had been replaced, buffed and polished. In short, it shone and gleamed like a new penny.

Rudolph stood proudly at the front, ready to lead his friends and the large group of 'agency' reindeer on their journey.

"Hic..."

"Uh oh!" Donner said from the back.

"CHOO!" completed Rudolph. "I wish I could shake off this cold," he commented, "It's really beginning to get under my fur."

"Or up your nose!" Prancer retorted from behind him.

After finishing what was left of his salad, Santa kissed Mrs Claus goodbye. She touched his cheek affectionately,

"Remember what I said, NO mince pies!"

Santa groaned, "Which leaves me with?"

Mary Claus smiled, and looked deliberately toward the door, "Rudolph's carrots!" she said loudly, knowing that our favourite reindeer would hear. The sound of chortling and the distinctive sound of a hairy hoof hitting the ground told her he had!

With his wife and the elves watching from the windows, Santa saluted them all and climbed aboard his brand new sleigh. "Here we go, boys!" Santa said, taking the reins and shaking them. The ecstatic reindeers and a smiling Santa took easily to the air. He waved at his family once more, and watched the Pole fade into the distance, as they began their journey.

Christmas was once again ON!

SPIRITS AND SLEUTHS

Hi, I'm Mia. Let me begin by telling you that I am not your average fifteen year old girl, in more ways than one. I listen to the Eagles and Fleetwood Mac and I don't do N-Dubz or Lady Gaga. It's my mother that waves Heat magazine under my nose! I have no interest in Katie and Peter's latest stunt! Mum and the kids at school think I'm weird. "Really, Mia, you should make some attempts to fit in!" Mum will say. "Why?" I reply simply and head back to my room. Anyway, I digress. Yes, I know words like 'digress', I learnt them from reading books. I don't wish to be mean, but it seems that half the kids in my class probably wouldn't even be able to spell it!

This story isn't about me, it's about my best friend Emma, or rather, her house. I guess you could say it's your average new build family home with three bedrooms and a fully fitted kitchen, blah, blah, blah! The estate agents' details said that there was 'room for the kids to play' and almost made a feature of the slide belonging to Emma's toddler twin sisters. Emma hated that! Actually, Emma hates them! They were an unexpected present, very much unexpected according to Emma, who is silently seething about having to leave her room behind when the family move somewhere bigger.

Sorry, where was I? Oh yes – the house. I have stayed there

lots of times but I've always felt uneasy. The first time I went in there four years ago, I felt so nauseous. Emma laughed and put it down to me eating too many of her Dad's dodgy pancakes! I didn't find it funny. She grabbed my hand and hauled me excitedly upstairs to see her new room. I remember suddenly not being able to breathe properly as we reached the doorway, and then being almost overwhelmed by the strong smell of smoke. I actually had to stop dead.

"You alright?" Emma turned to me, concerned. "You don't look too good." she asked, concerned.

"Has your Mum burnt something?" I replied quietly, my voice cracking slightly.

"No, not in the last twenty four hours!" Emma laughed, opening the door to show me her en suite. I think she expected me to be jealous, but I wasn't.

"Oh well, maybe the neighbours are having a bonfire or something then," I replied, and did my best to forget about it.

The day of Emma's fourteenth birthday, she asked me over for a barbeque. It was a Saturday, so Mum said yes when I asked to sleep over.

The house was icy cold when I stepped through the front door into the hall. It was the middle of August and sunlight was streaming through the windows. I had been comfortable in my short red summer dress, but suddenly I wished I had brought a jumper.

"Hello Mia!" Emma's mum said brightly as she carried a basket of washing downstairs "Oh Emma, for goodness sake, get Mia a drink! Don't just leave her standing there. She's walked all the way over here!" Emma grumbled and pulled me into the kitchen.

Leaning against the kitchen worktop, I was waiting for my best friend to fill up our glasses with Coke when I clearly saw a little boy run towards the back door, from the direction of the hall. He looked about our age and had ash blonde hair, appearing not just once, but twice, as the scene repeated itself again.

My heart stopped beating for a second, and my blood ran cold in my veins. "Em!" I whispered, almost too scared to speak, "Did you see that?"

"See what?" she replied, handing me the glass. I struggled to take it from her because my hands were clammy and trembling,

"Um... you won't believe this but I think I just saw a ghost! It was a little boy in dark brown trousers and a white shirt. He just ran across there!" I said, gesturing towards the back door. Emma put her arm round me and giggled.

"Oh yeah, right, you see dead people! You need help Mee!" she commented, and giggled again.

Up until then I had doubted myself, believing that everything I felt and even smelt in that house was a product of the overactive imagination that my Mum says I get from Gran. Still shaking, I took hold of Emma's arm, "Come on, we're going outside!" I said, rather more urgently than I had intended. Once out on the lawn I felt safe again and the goose pimples began to disappear.

****

I remember being reluctant to stay that night, and I didn't sleep a wink! I was 'top to toe' with Emma, who snuffled and shuffled most of the night, frequently pulling the Justin Bieber covered duvet completely off me. At about two in the morning, I needed the loo. Closing my eyes and counting to a hundred, I tried not to think about it. Eventually, I had to give in and make my way across the landing to the bathroom. With every click of the pipe work or creaking of floorboard, the latter of which was of my own making, I jumped out of my skin and looked nervously around me.

I was tiptoeing back past the twins' room a few minutes later, when I noticed a hazy red mist floating steadily up the staircase. Suddenly I no longer cared about waking anyone up and bolted back to bed as fast as my legs would carry me! Emma stirred momentarily as I pulled the duvet roughly over my head. There I stayed, huddled tightly and listening to my own breathing, until the birds finally started to sing.

I was picked up just after breakfast, and when I'd hugged Emma goodbye, I asked Mum to drop me at the library. She sighed and rolled her eyes, "What do you want to go there for? We've got the internet at home!" When I persisted, she did as I asked, telling me to ring when I was ready to come home.

I enjoy the peace of the library. I love the quiet industriousness of it, and the hissed "Sshhh!" every time someone's mobile accidentally rings! I turned mine off, and began to search the 'Local History' section. I found lots on industry and the Civil War but that wasn't what was needed. Sipping some squash that I quickly smuggled out of my bag, I looked around. Just about to give up, I noticed the librarian and wandered nervously over to her. She was busy on the computer but she looked up and smiled warmly.

"Excuse me" I muttered quietly "I don't suppose you would know anything about the housing estate on Wilmhurst Lane, would you? It's just I can't seem to find anything."

The woman had red hair and when she smiled at me, her green eyes twinkled. Not at all the way you'd expect a librarian to look.

"This way," she replied, "the estate used to be fields with a few smallholdings. My grandfather was born there." She showed me to a big pile of newspapers tucked away on a bottom shelf. "No one asks to look at these much," she said almost apologetically. "There are some old maps over in the corner. You should find what you are looking for and if you need any help, I'm just over here."

I thanked her and, feeling like Sherlock Holmes with a wonderful buzz I can't explain, I began trawling through facsimiles, papers and maps. Time flew by. I was propelled by thoughts of Emma's house and the field it was built on. I grinned to myself. Heat magazine couldn't give you this type of buzz!

Sometime after lunch, I struck gold! With a map that showed the location of 'Little Croft smallholding' at my side, I found a front page story dated March 1910. "Hamsworth Family Die in Fire Tragedy." I felt sad. That would explain the red mist and the little boy running toward the door. Despite myself, I let out a tiny squeal of delight and everyone turned to look at me. I shrank down in my seat, embarrassed. From her place behind the desk the librarian looked in my direction and smiled.

On the way out of the library a while later, I filled out a membership form. When the librarian took it from me, she looked at my name in its black block capitals.
"Well, hello Miss Woodward," she said, "glad to see you have

such an interest in books!" Her eyes made their way slowly down the form, checking for errors as she spoke "Don't forget if there's ever a book you can't find, just come up to the desk and ask. I've been here long enough to know where most things are."

I smiled, and, thanking her, turning to make my way towards the exit. However, as I walked through the heavy doors and out into the street, the woman's voice seemed to follow behind me, "Just ask for Lucy, Lucy Hamsworth. They will know who you mean…"

THE KEEPSAKE

Sometimes I feel like a hamster, running round and round on her wheel. There is no time for anything else! Ideally, of course, I'd be the type of hamster who didn't bother with her wheel at all. I like to think of myself as a 'free spirit' – or at least I did when I was younger. I would allow myself time to stop and enjoy the little pleasures of life. I would NEVER become bogged down by the day-to-day drudgery – or so I thought! Now, I have a husband, two daughters and a job. The hamster wheel is my world.

Last Saturday, with my husband at work and our twelve year old twins squabbling over something at high pitched volume, I sought refuge in the garage. I'd been meaning to clean it out since I don't know when, and now seemed as good a time as any!

Lifting the garage door I was hit by the smell of old engine oil, paint and dust. When was the last time anyone came in here anyway? Feeling my way through the darkness, I reached the light switch and pulled it. The hanging bulb hesitated for a few seconds and then flickered reluctantly, as if it had been woken from a deep sleep.

Under the eerie yellow light I could make out a mountain of boxes pushed against the back wall, a pile of rags, an old bike separated from its front wheel and some paint cans. Seemingly everything we had ever planned to take to the tip, mend or give to a charity shop was in here, strewn haphazardly on the concrete floor. I sighed and wished I'd never opened the door!

In the background, the girls were still arguing. Knowing that they would come to some agreement about whatever it was by themselves eventually, I decided I was better off staying out here. If I got involved it would lead to one or other of them in an all-day sulk or cries of "You always take her side!" Apart from anything else, I wasn't sure how many more enraged slams the bedroom doors could take – and they weren't even teenagers yet! 'I'll go in if there's blood,' I thought, shifting the first box.

I'd lost count of the amount of creatures that had crawled out of the family debris even within the first hour! I remember my husband's reluctance to tackle the job at all came from a particularly bad encounter with a spider that he swore was the size of his hand! "I'm not going back in there unless some sort of spider exorcist goes in first!" That was five years ago and true to his word, he hadn't!

While tidying up, I was aware that my mind was only half on the job in hand. The other half was rushing through things I hadn't managed to finish at work. Phone calls that weren't made, people I hadn't managed to speak to on Friday – and looking at the mess strewn before me on the floor reminded me of my desk!

There was a time when Friday afternoon was Friday afternoon! I could close the door and happily leave everything there until Monday. My weekends were my own –before husband and children; before meetings, expectations, mortgages, football matches, and dance classes. Wait. Damn it! Dance classes!

"POPPY!" I yelled, almost dumping a box on my foot as I headed for the door. "Poppy! You've got dance class! Get in the car now! Grace, hurry up!"
Standing in the hallway, I caught a glimpse of myself in the mirror. My hands were on my hips, my face was all red and I looked like I hadn't slept for a week. Oh God, I was... MY MOTHER! It was like somebody deflated a balloon inside me. Free spirit? Ha! That was all gone with the idealism of youth. I was bound to my hamster's wheel.

Poppy was in front of me now, waiting to go, and Grace stood behind her, pouting as usual. "Poppy, do you want to go to dance class? You don't have to go today. You don't have to go any day." I didn't know what had come over me, but suddenly I felt guilty for taking Poppy to any sort of 'class' at the weekends – even though it had been her choice.

Poppy rolled her eyes, "Oh Mum...can we just GO"?!

I felt better. "Okay", I replied, and headed for the car.

The hour spent waiting for the lesson to finish passed more quickly than usual. We had dropped Grace off at a friend's house on the way – even managing to get a smile out of her! Sitting in the car alone, the silence was bliss. I watched the sun dance freely on the dashboard, and thought of my father.

He always said he wanted a small boat when he retired. All he wanted was to sit and drink tea on the river, while watching the sun reflecting off the water. He loved the peace and was waiting patiently for the day he could do that to his heart's content. With tears in my eyes I wished he'd made it. It was a shock when he died suddenly with only a year to go. Watching the sun again, I thought of his words to me on my twenty-first birthday. "Don't rush, time passes quickly enough. The clock is always ticking, my love, but you can stand still occasionally."

The girls were quiet that evening. Poppy was practising a ballet move on the hall floor with her iPod in her ears. She was in a world of her own. I watched as her pair of pink ballet shoes came skipping past me over and over. For a while I watched her face. She was perfectly happy and while she was dancing, it was like nothing else existed for her.

Grace had cheered up, too. She was sitting on the stairs with the phone attached to her ear and if I wasn't mistaken, my formerly sourpuss daughter was giggling! Maybe I was doing something right after all. When she saw me coming towards her she mouthed the words "five more minutes Mum". Shrugging my shoulders, I smiled at her and went outside to the garage.

It had to be here somewhere, I thought, rummaging through the boxes, some of which we hadn't touched since we moved in. I felt an overwhelming sense of guilt because it shouldn't be in here at all. It belonged somewhere safe. Eventually at the bottom of a cardboard box that was still partially sealed with faded packing tape, I found it. A small blue velvet case, still soft on top but slightly worn now. The lid popped open with that distinctive sound you get with small jewellery or keepsake boxes. I peered inside at the silver clock attached to a fob. The hands had stopped moving at twenty to four on a day long gone by. Carefully, I turned over the watch and read the engraving made by a skilled hand:

'In case you forget. Happy 21st, Dad.'

DAISY'S STORY – A CAT'S TALE

I guess I've come pretty far in the last nine years. I think my name should be 'Lucky' instead of Daisy. My first humans were very nasty to me. I know I will never forget it.

The man had a temper, and he would often shout at me. But worse than that, he had big boots and would kick me when he was angry. There were days when he would pick me up and throw me if I got in the way. I was just a baby. I didn't know what I had done wrong, and I had tried so hard to make him like me.

Then one day, when I was about five months old, a lady came to get me. I was trembling and for a while I thought she was going to hurt me too, but she didn't. Instead, she took me away to a quiet, warm place, and promised me softly that she would find me a home; a proper one, where someone would love me. I didn't know what a 'home' was, but I looked forward to it.

Time passed, and then at last, a man with glasses came to see me. I made a fuss of him. Even though I was trembling with fear, and nervous around his big shoes, I managed to let him stroke me. I pushed my small body into his hands, and wanted him to take me 'home'. I felt sad when he stood up and left.

The next evening, the lady I was staying with bent down and spoke to me. "Come on Daisy; let's take you to your new home." Home? I really had a home! I was happy, but very frightened, and my tummy was still hurting from where the nasty man had used me as a football.

On the way to my new home I fell asleep in my basket. I was woken up by a pair of gentle hands lifting me out, careful not to touch my tummy. I was so grateful, but all of a sudden I was struck by fear again. I panicked, and scratched the hand. I didn't mean it, and I hoped they knew that.

When the new human put me down, I was immediately aware of the space. I had never seen so much room. A far cry from my tiny basket! Part of me wanted to explore, and learn all the new sights and smells around me. One of which was a smell I would later become very used to – that of burnt food! Somebody couldn't cook!

Anyway, as I stood there on the cold tiles of the kitchen floor, I felt panic well up inside me again. I was desperate to be safe, so I ran for the nearest, darkest place I could find - under the sink.

For the longest time, I just sat there, cowering. They put food down for me, but I wouldn't come out until I heard the door slam, and I was sure there was no one around. I would eat, drink, and then retreat back to my hiding place. For about two weeks I stayed there.

Often the new humans would come and peer in at me. They would stay a while, call my name, and then I would watch their feet pass as they left me again. I recognised one pair of shoes. They belonged to the man with glasses that had visited me. I was still nervous though, even though I really did try not to be. Something in me just wouldn't let me move.

Apart from him, there was a bossy woman with clunky shoes, who wore lots of lipstick and was definitely in charge! A younger blonde girl was there too. She had big feet, and laughed a lot. She made too much noise, and frightened me all over again.

Then there was her.

She was small and had the quietest voice. She talked to me gently as she struggled around the kitchen. I listened to her voice, its tone, rising and falling, and I felt comforted. Late one night when everyone else had gone to bed, she came again, with a dish of milk, and lay down flat on her tummy. She stayed there talking softly in the dark, tempting, calling and whispering.

Suddenly, I knew everything would be okay and that she would protect me. When I was sure it was safe, I came out slowly and drank some milk. Her shaking hand reached forward and stroked me. It really would be alright, as long as I was with her. I noticed a scratch on her hand, and felt sorry.

I followed her at first up to her bedroom, and then, as my confidence grew, I went everywhere with her. In time, I knew I was safe in that room. I began to lie on the bed with my tummy exposed for the first time, and I even let her rub it – for a second or so!

She would talk to me about everything, and I began to show myself to her more. She had a horrible yellow quilt cover that I would lie on. It was too bright, but she thought it was "cool".

Having always been a sickly cat, I expressed my displeasure by throwing up on it at every given opportunity! I could always blame it on a fur ball! When she got cross, I would curl myself up and look at her as if butter wouldn't melt in my mouth! She was putty in my paws!

Some days we would play, when it was just us. She would roll up a ball of paper and throw it for me. I realised that she couldn't move as easily as the others, and that there were days when she was hurting, so I helped her by kicking the paper back towards her and then picking it up in my teeth and carrying nearer to her. She told me I was a "clever girl". She's right, I am!

She is the best human in the world. I know she is not as brave or confident as she makes herself out to be. When she cries, I sit with her and offer a paw to smooth.

Not so long ago, things changed. A tall man started coming to visit. I think he must be her Tom Cat! He has a soft voice and he looks at her like I do, with love. He strokes me and is nice to me, which is just as well because no Tom Cat comes between me and her - ever!

Now though, I don't see as much of her as I would like to. You see, when the Tom Cat touches me, his eyes go all red and blotchy. Oh, and he sneezes! It's not my fault! I just like to keep my black and white fur clean and beautiful! I know she misses me and I miss her too, very much. But, she always told me how much she wanted a Tom Cat to love her, and now she has one! I am happy for her.

Anyway, the point of me talking to you today is to tell you my story. I was lucky to find a human like her. She changed my life, but I think I have changed hers too. I am, and I always will be, her baby.

SHARING TIME: (BASED ON A DIARY ENTRY)

Eva's tiny hand curls around my finger unquestioningly. It is perfect and warm.

Settling back against a cushion, I look down into her sleeping face. A moment of peace washes over me. I realise that this is where I'm meant to be, and know that I couldn't be happier if I were part of sunlight itself.

The only sound is gentle breathing as she slumbers, and for a moment everything seems still.

"Well, I guess I'd better take her home..." The voice of my best friend shatters my illusion so forcefully that I actually feel it crumble around me.

For a while the baby was mine, and I glimpsed into a world that I know I will never be part of. The bond between mother and child is one that I will never share.

"Yes you'd better," I say, shaking myself from my reverie. Handing the bundle over, the tiny hand is torn reluctantly from mine, and the last link is severed.

"I'll bring her over again soon" my best friend says quietly, as she takes the little girl fully into her loving arm. With the other, she reaches across to hug me.

I struggle with every fibre of my being not to resent her. I know it is not her fault that I can't ever have a baby.

I feel glad that she is happy and since Eva's birth, there is a new contentment about her, and a light in her eyes. Despite the lack of sleep, she looks serene, and finally complete. With one finger, I stroke the baby's cheek, and whisper "goodbye..."

When the door closes, I feel empty and cold. Leaning back against the solid frame, the unshed tears roll down my face.

SECTION THREE: SELECTED ARTICLES, & ALL THINGS RANDOM!

PART OF ME WISHES FOR SNOW

Part of me wishes for snow. I love it when the world is covered in a white blanket, the warm tones of earth resting beneath.

I like to think that everything sleeps sometimes, but nature never sleeps. Instead it's always striving. Colours and textures go on changing - from the falling of leaves to the bareness of trees, as another year passes by.

Part of me wishes for snow, because everything seems calm and timeless. I love to watch it fall from the night sky, like tiny gentle feathers. It feels like they float freely and land where they want to. It must be nice to do that. Until daylight, no one will stand on it; destroying the blanket with large, lasting footprints. Steps that are taken for granted.

Part of me wishes for snow, so that the Christmas lights reflect off it, and the firelight seems to burn brighter. Outside, nature carries on but I don't have to see it. I don't have to think about new lives beginning, sprouting afresh, the way nature is supposed to do.

Part of me wishes for snow, because I need that blanket too. I need to see civilisation stop, on the surface anyway. Stop striving, fighting, moving forward, making money.

Everything that is usually at the edges of my vision has temporarily disappeared.

The world is at my level. It's flat and equal while we share the white blanket. No one else can move properly either! I can hear laughter and watch a snowball fight from the window. I love my hands around a mug of hot chocolate, and who knows? Maybe we'll toast marshmallows! I love the simple things, and outside, for now so do they. The world is mine, tonight.

SUNSHINE AND DRIZZLE CAKE

I was in pain when I woke up. My hips were throbbing and a sharpness was surging through my sides. Shifting on my back, I wondered if it was too late to cancel our plans. I couldn't guarantee I wasn't going to be sick again.

My husband peered around the bedroom door, "How are you feeling? If you want to cancel we'd better do it soon..."

Bright, beautiful sunshine was streaming through the window, and knowing how rare it had been this summer, I responded with, "No, I'm okay".

I wanted to be up, out and taking photos of a church we hadn't been to yet. It might seem a strange hobby (especially for an atheist) but I love taking photos of churches almost as much as I love taking photos of derelict buildings!

Churches and the graveyards that surround them are special to me. It's the architecture, the history, but most importantly, it's the peace and the stillness. There is a calming effect whether you believe in 'anything else' or not. Churches rarely change so the feeling of timelessness is another thing that attracts me.

Imagine all those people for all those generations that have pushed open that heavy door...

I didn't bother with breakfast - I rarely do. The 'Endo' makes me feel to sick in the mornings. Instead I swallowed a painkiller and sipped a cup of tea. Tea is my 'starter fuel' and feeling sick or not, I find I don't function well without it!

My husband's sister arrived and gave me a hug. We watched our husbands load my wheelchair into the back of their new car.

"I hope it fits" she said, smiling at me.

"Me too," I replied as another pain shot through my hip and down to my toes.

It did.

Mells church (the church of St Andrew) is especially pretty. I'll include its Wikipedia link so you can see it for yourself, but I loved the porch with its window, that you can see above the outer door. Also, the interior is especially ornate: so much detail and unique memorials, one of which was designed by Edwin Lutyens.

The graveyard has several notable burials, perhaps the most notable is Siegfried Sassoon (1886 - 1967), the war poet and soldier. I'll put his wiki page below too:

With my wheelchair parked beside his grave (the churchyard is too bumpy to push the wheelchair over and I definitely was not in a fit state to walk even a little way on my crutches), I wondered about all the things he must have seen. That has to change a person.

The writer in me wondered about his writing process, and if he had a desk! I don't have one - usually it's the dining room table or my notebook comes to bed with me...

I shivered a bit as the pain ran through me again...but nothing compared to what people involved in war must experience. I felt lucky.

Mells is quite close to us. It's a beautiful village with old cottages, a post office, pub and a few tea rooms. The place is riddled with history, and I believe the nursery rhyme 'Little Jack Horner' has its origins there. The Horner's being local wealthy landowners, and responsible for bringing many 'arty types' to the village.

The sunshine made my pain seem less important, and as I sat on the wooden outdoor chairs of The Walled Garden with the warmth on my back, I knew I'd done the right thing in forcing myself to go out. It is a case of forcing myself sometimes; what with the pain, nausea and depression, it can be easier to just stay at home with my husband and let the days slip by.

The lemon drizzle cake sweet on my tongue, the sunshine and my husband's hand in mine, made me so glad that this one hadn't.

I HATE BRAS!

I hate bras! It's not that they are uncomfortable - although they can be, especially if an underwire digs in! Ooh, don't!

It's the expectation that women HAVE to wear them. Now, obviously this is not a new idea, but I'm going to say it anyway. If a woman doesn't wear a bra, people look at her differently (and not just because she's got 'em hanging free). There is something extra attached.

A woman is a slut, or easy, or has no pride in her appearance. I don't know what it is; a mixture of many things - but it pisses me off! I didn't wear a bra for years (until recently) because I felt so strongly about this issue. It was my own small act of rebellion.

Who the hell has the right to judge me, or tell me what I should and shouldn't wear?!

Now, most women wear them for support, and that's fine. It's necessary for comfort or whatever in many cases. That's a separate issue though, I think - and yes, it's the reason why I started wearing them again - but I still hate it!

Don't go thinking either, that wearing a bra is going to help you stop 'sagging' - (well, it might for a while - or at least make them look better), but things inevitably...go downwards! Of course you look better when you're wearing them -

especially when you put on a little weight like I have! But I still hate them! I object to the whole thing! After all, you don't see men wearing them to carry around their MOOBS do you?! (Well, not that I've seen any way!)

Why should men be allowed to be 'free,' but women be restricted? It's the same in a lot of issues, not just bras!

Yes, attitudes towards women have changed - and they've moved forward a lot, especially since the contraceptive pill became available. Women have a lot more freedom and that's the greatest thing, but why should we be told what to do anyway?!

I'm sorry, but until I don't feel obligated to wear one or judged if I go out without one, things haven't moved forward enough!

SHE'S NOT IN FASHION

Some of my pet hates (I have several), are beauty standards, and the 'fashion' industry.

I mean, please! Who the hell has any right to decide what's beautiful and what's not? Or what's 'in' and what's not?! Who died and made fashion designers arbiters of good taste?! Half the things that are so-called 'fashionable', I wouldn't be seen dead in! How dare anybody tell me what I should and shouldn't be wearing?!

It's what's on the inside of a person that counts, not what they look like, or which 'designer label' they are wearing. If you're anything like me, though, you'll probably end up spilling orange juice or cake down it on its second outing! Having said that, if it really makes you feel better to spend a fortune on a piece of clothing that will be 'out of date' in twelve months, then do it.

The fashion industry often makes people feel that they have to be a certain weight, or look a certain way, to be considered 'attractive' or 'good enough', and that's rubbish! Being 'attractive' is as about confidence, I think, as much as anything else. Once you've come to terms with who you are, and you 'own' your imperfections and faults, what people see matters less. It's about being comfortable in your own skin.

I won't pretend to be the most confident person in the world. I'm not. There are times when I'm plagued by self-doubt, but it's been a fair while since that extended to how I look. Now, I just accept that there are some things about myself I can't change - but it took me a very long time to get here.

Having a disability - I have Cerebral Palsy - immediately makes you different, (at least in a lot of people's eyes). I wasn't meant to 'fit in', and maybe to a certain extent, that has helped me. It's easier to follow your own path when you're on a different one to start with!

I'm not saying it's easy. When I was a teenager, I worried terribly about my weight. Then again, in my early twenties. And I'd be lying if I told you that I'm completely free of that, but the only reason I worry about my weight now is a practical one, not emotional.

If I gain too much weight, my mobility will become even more restricted. My hips and knees will need replacing at a much earlier stage than I'm ready for.

I know those operations will have to happen sooner or later, due to the 'wear and tear' that goes with Cerebral Palsy, but I've spent enough time in hospital to know that I will do anything I can to avoid going back there too soon!

As a teenager too, I had all the teenage angst - 'will anybody ever want me?' 'Oooh, I really hate my hair' - and that was compounded by the worry that boys (and later, men) wouldn't be able to see past the disability, and just see me.

Disability is a lot to come to terms with; it's even harder when you're battling depression, and you've got all the teenage hormones flying through your system. I won't pretend I've entirely come to terms with my disability and the limitations placed on my life, either, but I'm further along that road than I ever thought I would be.

I know who I am now, and maybe that's why I don't feel the need to worry about make-up or fashion.

It's not that I don't take pride in my appearance. I love shopping for brightly coloured tunic tops. I feel comfortable and relaxed in those, and that's my point. You don't need to be governed by what society tells you is attractive, fashionable or will give you a certain status. You just have to learn to accept yourself, and wear what makes you feel good. If that IS keeping up to date with the latest fashion, wearing expensive make-up, and having a designer handbag, then go for it, but what I'm saying is it doesn't have to be!

You have nothing to prove to anyone: not your friends, not your family, and definitely not society! Fashion is fleeting, and so is life. Do what makes you happy inside and makes you glad to wake up every morning.

Don't spend your time worrying about what the people think of you, because they won't remember what you were wearing, or how you looked, but they will remember who you are!

ABANDONED - WHY I LOVE DERELICT BUILDINGS

People tell me my love of derelict and abandoned buildings, (well any place that's abandoned, really) is strange. I think people who don't love them are strange!

What is there to love? Everything! It's the history, the peace, the mystery, the calm and lots more besides!

Who was the last person to stand in here? Who was the last person to lock up and go?

Who put such-and-such on the floor and left it there?

What was this place like when it was 'alive' with people?

That's another thing – people make the mistake of thinking that a deserted building is dead and meaningless. It isn't. Even the decay process itself is beautiful, if you choose to see it that way. All those changes, colours, textures - and once again, the history.

What gives anyone the right to destroy something that has been there so long? Improve it, bring it back to life. Don't make it disappear, then act as if it never existed. Don't replace it with something ugly and modern, just because you can make money from it!

Money isn't everything!

If we don't protect these places, and protect our past, how

can we learn from it?

I'm not saying that we must keep everything. Some things have to go, especially if they are dangerous. The point is, why let them get to that state?

Maybe I'm being too much of an idealist. We all know that money is a big issue. They say 'money makes the world go round', but it doesn't have to - not always!

All I'm asking is for a bit of thought when you walk past one. Let your imagination run wild a little. Then, I hope, you will see what I mean.

I've lost count of the windows I've peered through, and the places I've wished I could get inside, like some do. With my difficulties, I can't, of course - but I can dream, and I can do so much wonderful research.

There are so many beautiful pictures online, taken by people who have the guts to squeeze through gaps, under things, and over things, so that these lost treasures can be documented, shared, and kept (in a lot of cases, long after the building itself has been destroyed).

It's not always safe and it's not always legal, but urban exploration (or 'urbexing' for short), is a growing phenomenon, and I think it's a necessary one.

I can't describe the feeling I get from looking at abandoned buildings. I get excited, like a kid in a sweet shop! I feel light, and happy. It gives me a buzz similar to the one I get from writing, or singing.

These places are special. They are frozen in time, and they belong to a world that doesn't exist anymore. With everything around us changing so fast, and everyone struggling to keep up, shouldn't we be keeping pieces of our history?

Once they are gone, they cannot ever be replaced.

People loved these places once, and luckily, some of us still do.

DISABILITY AND EMPATHY

As I sit here, the pain is ripping through my body. It is relentless, like waves hitting rocks on a stormy day and I'm writing this off the cuff as it were, purely as a distraction. I want it to stop. I feel like something evil is gnawing on my muscles and positively relishing it! Painkillers will take the edge off... for about half an hour.

I guess I should've known yesterday that today would be worse. I was aching you see – aching badly. But I still wanted to go for a walk because the sun was out. My husband lovingly calls me 'the hermit' and I wanted to prove him wrong.

Every physio I have ever had told me I need exercise, especially since my pulmonary embolism in 2005. I have to stay as active and fit as I can, but it is so hard to stay motivated and keep going when you know that it will hurt later, if it doesn't already.
It drains my energy so quickly. Sometimes I feel like a car running on empty. I have to carry on but there is no fuel left, I have nothing left to give.

As a side note, I often get this feeling about my friendships. Part of my personality is that I am there for everybody, whenever they need me. My husband calls it my 'saintliness' but it is just the way I am.

On days like today though, I admit to seeing their trivial little worries as exactly that, and hate myself for it. He often reminds me that very few of them have been there for me. "Isn't that just the way it is though?" I'll say, and he will roll his eyes. He's wonderful! He reminds me that I have enough to deal with!

The thing is, my disability has probably made me more empathetic and more in tune with people. So yeah, thanks for that! I'm not saying I am an angel. I can be horribly moody and sometimes very depressed. That is just life. Everybody gets depressed and everybody has tough times, but it is how you get through it that matters.

The pain is no better, and despite having enjoyed talking to you (please forgive my disjointed ramblings) I still want to throw something out of sheer frustration! Yes, I admit it, there is a bit of self-pity mixed in today too, because I did not ask for this, and there is no 'end' for me like there is for others with problems. There is no solution.

But I will not give up, EVER, even though right now part of me wants to. I have an amazing husband and a very strong marriage. I have my family and I have my writing.
When I finish typing I will go and curl up in my husband's arms and I might even finally cry, but I know that all this HAS

made me stronger. I hope it continues to do so.

What I'm trying to say is that even when it doesn't feel like it, even when it seems like there is just too much pain, you can always find a little strength from somewhere.

Please don't give up.

DEPRESSION: THE HAND AROUND YOUR ANKLE

I've been asked, a lot, 'what is depression like?'

Usually, I would describe it like a hole that you can't quite get yourself out of, but I think, maybe this might explain it a little better:

It's like you're in water, and everyone else is swimming happily around you, but someone or something has a hold of your ankle and is pulling you under, even though you're fighting with everything you've got to stay afloat.

The harder you fight, the more desperate and tired you get. You know you should be swimming happily too, like other people are, and you feel so guilty that you can't get away. So you find yourself, flapping your arms around and pretending to be like them.

You don't want the people you love to look over and see you drowning, but you can't break free of the hand that's pulling you under. Over time, it becomes a battle of wills. If you can just keep your head above water a little bit longer, then the hand around your ankle will get tired before you do, and gradually loosen the grip...

It isn't simple, and maybe I over simplify things a bit here.

There are times, even when you've begun the 'swim' back,

that the hand will feel like it's going to grab you again. However, you can keep your head above water - you know you can.

When people have almost drowned, they often describe a surge of superhuman strength that stopped them going under the water. It's not easy when you're so tired that you can't see tomorrow, and you're so sick of feeling pain that you just want it to stop.

That's when you need to find it the most. Try to tread water, and keep your head up, for five more minutes; one more hour; or one more day, even.

In time, the hand around your ankle will loosen.

Depression is an illness, and you should never forget that. It is not your fault that you've found yourself here. It's perfectly okay to ask for help, because everybody needs help sometimes. It's nothing to be ashamed of, I promise.

Just try to keep swimming. You are not alone.

CAN'T COOK, WON'T COOK!

Somebody made the mistake of asking me my thoughts on cooking. My response was this:

'Well, I guess we all have to eat'!

The poor unsuspecting person then listened patiently while I 'went off on one', or to put it more politely... ahem, 'outlined the issues I'm about to cover in this piece'!

My husband has always said that he would be much happier if we could get the nutrients we need to live from just taking a pill. He doesn't see food, the cooking or ingestion of it, as a pleasurable experience. He eats to get the right nutrients, to be healthy; but this isn't about him, it's about me.

I find cooking difficult, complicated by the fact that (being disabled) I always need to use one hand to balance myself, and I can't stand up for long without pain. So cooking is something I will willingly hand over to someone else!

My few attempts have either resulted in injury, pain, or late night trips to the chip shop! If I'm really unlucky, I get all three on the same night!

People often don't think about how difficult an everyday task (such as cooking) can be for a disabled person. They tend to take their ability to manage for granted. For a disabled person, the smallest of tasks takes more planning, time, and energy. Energy which many of us don't have, in the first place!

Speaking for myself, even if it were possible for me to stand without pain and use both hands, I would still have trouble lifting heavy saucepans for example, or bending down to take hot food from the oven.

Due to the slight tremor in my hands (due to Cerebral Palsy), I don't feel very safe, and whilst I might be able to prepare vegetables (sitting down), the tremor is a problem after a while, as is the pain from the tension in my wrists.

As I said, I may be able to manage as a one off but to do it regularly would be too much for me. As a quick side note, this is why being able to do things in a 'safe, reliable, and timely manner' needs to stay in the criteria for disability benefits. (You never know these days whether it could be removed again!) You see, it might be okay to do it once, but that doesn't mean I could do it whenever I needed to eat!

In writing this piece, I began to think about whether I would actually like to cook, if I could manage it without the hassle and pain? Eventually I came to the conclusion that I wouldn't! You spend ages doing preparation, following recipes (if you are so inclined) and then you have to loiter around to make sure that it doesn't burn. After all that time and stress, it is gulped down in five minutes flat, and you're left with plates to clean.

I wouldn't mind so much if it was just a one off, but no, you have to do it all again the next day, and every day after that!

You might have gathered from this that domesticity is not my strong point! I tend to think, along with many others, that I have better things to do with my time. Having said that, I also think it's quite sad that cooking a meal from scratch is being lost due to microwaves and 'quick' foods.

Lifestyles are different now, though. Few people have the time to make things from scratch, and with the cost of food (and living in general) having risen, while wages have stagnated (and vital benefits have been cut), few people have the money to eat what my Gran would've called 'proper food' anyway. So it's no wonder things are different.

Mum is not a fan of cooking either. I'm like her, in that I am impatient with such things, so when I lived at home I wasn't really taught - although one of my earliest memories is sitting on the kitchen worktop, 'helping' mum make gingerbread men and being allowed to lick the spoons afterwards. That's a point; maybe if it were possible to live entirely on cake mix, I'd be more interested! Although that's doubtful!

I was beginning to think that my husband might have the right idea, - let's all just pop a pill and have done with it. However, that would mean no more chocolate cake, and strangely enough, I've changed my mind!

HELEN... ON ICE

Is it true that I own a pair of figure skates, even though I'll never be able to use them because I can't walk, or even stand unaided, never mind skate?

Yes!

They are white, professional figure skates; properly laced, and in their box. I've never really known why it was important to me that I have them, but it is. My mum told me once about a blind boy that she used to teach. His obsession was maps. Even though he couldn't see them, and would never use them, he collected them like his life depended on it. Figure skating and dance are both lifelong passions. I read rule books, and notice things that someone who just watched it for 'fun' would not.

I can tell by the speed a skater takes a jump, or by their position in the air, if they are going to land successfully or fall.

Why do I love it so much? I guess because it's artistic, technical, and creative, but also because it symbolises something. It's about freedom, and it's about moving the body in ways that I can't and never have been able to.

I love the glide, and I think that one of the best sounds in the world is the swish of blades on ice. It sounds almost like music to me, and I could listen to it all day. I love ice rinks. I love the sheen on them if you go early in the morning, and the shiver you get when you first walk into one.

I love the first moments after the Zamboni has removed the top layer, and the rink looks so perfect. I always envy the first person who will set their blades on ice, and make 'tramlines'. I wish that those tramlines were mine - because in another life, they would've been.

HELEN...ON WRITING

It's difficult to explain how I write to anyone else, because it tends to vary depending on my mood and also where I am. Before I get started on that, however, I'd better try and explain why I write.

To be honest, I don't remember a time when I didn't. When I was about six or seven, I developed an interest in history, after a family holiday to France. We visited some of the chateaux in the Loire valley, and I wanted to know everything! Who lived there, when, why?

Something in my imagination was sparked. It wasn't that I wanted to be a princess and live in them myself. It was an interest in what had been there, and who. After we visited her room in Chateau de Chenonceau, I was fascinated by the life of Catherine de Medici. When we arrived home, I asked my Mum to find out more about her. I was far too young to do research myself, so Mum did it for me, and made notes. I then began to write about Catherine's life in a dark green exercise book. I guess you could say that was my first 'book' of sorts.

I realised that I loved writing. I loved the feeling that I could fill the paper - and only me - my way.
I was also aware that I wasn't like other children. It wasn't

possible for me to run, jump, skip, and play in the way that they did. I could write, though, and I had all these ideas and questions and colourful things coming into my mind, so I wrote them down.

A year later, Mum and I worked on another book, only this time I wrote about Mary, Queen of Scots. Through mum, and the way she was reading and finding things out from different books, I learnt the importance of research and opinions. She would say to me, 'Well, this book thinks such and such, but this book thinks...'

So that stayed with me, and along with it, a love of research, information, and randomness! I'm a very curious person, as I think most writers are.

I started writing because it was a natural progression, as part of other interests, and something to do, but then magic happened - and words are magic!

The realisation that I could create worlds, stories and characters, as well as express my feelings, became part of who I am over time. It became an escape from whatever I was going through and a way to focus on the positives, too. Writing is like being in another world, and when the words come, it's like nothing else exists. I love that. I love knowing that I can create anything, and the buzz that happens as I do it, and when something is completed, is like a drug!

There is a sense of excitement, of happiness, that I can get in few other ways.

It is my constant, my passion, my ability, and being able to do it, makes up (at least in some ways) for all the things I can't do, and it can never be taken away from me.

As for process, that's where it gets tricky, because there isn't one single way.

I always carry a notebook with me because the smallest thing will give me an idea. Things like leaves floating, sounds of engines, snippets of conversation, debate, graffiti on toilet walls, movement, scents, music, anything!

I can't pretend it happens as often as it used to. It seems to happen in phases now and then disappears for a while, leaving me in a state of panic, mixed with an almost palpable feeling of loss. Doubting myself, and worrying that each piece I write, might be my last.

After all this time, what would I be without it? I can't imagine that, and I don't want to! It would be like ripping my heart out.

Usually, I will write the first draft of something in the notebook, and then edit it - also in the notebook. I like being able to see something taking shape. That is in danger of being lost, as we use computers more and more, and are able to delete something we aren't happy with. We are in danger of losing the spark, and freshness, if we are constantly getting rid of things, because we feel they aren't right.

After a draft, or two, I will then make a decision about what I do with it. Is it strong enough for a blog? Would somebody else get more out of it? Is it good enough to be read at all? Sometimes it takes me a while to make that decision, and others, it will be instant, but I rarely throw anything away.

Even when something appears completed, it often isn't. I will find a better word, or think of something that I have left out, so it takes a lot for me to say 'yes, okay, that's done'.

Whatever happens in the future, wherever I am, whatever I'm doing or feeling, I know I will never be alone, because for as long as I have my words, I have somewhere to go.

THANK YOU

To those
Who cared enough,
To wear their hearts
Upon their sleeves,
I thank you,
For saving me.

And to those
Who held me close,
When all I could do
Was cry,
I thank you,
And I smile.

To those
Who stayed
When others went,
I can never tell you
How much,
That meant.

And to those
Who gave comfort,
In my hour of need
I ask you now,
To laugh
With me.

To those
Who were there,
When I fell apart
I thank you now
And give you,

My heart.

Made in the USA
Charleston, SC
26 May 2016